GA...
BOS...
PLAY

D0896602

Kelen

GAMES BOSSES PLAY

**36 Career Busters
Your Supervisor May Be
Firing Your Way and How
You Can Defend Yourself**

RUSSELL WILD

CB
CONTEMPORARY BOOKS

Library of Congress Cataloging-in-Publication Data

Wild, Russell.
    Games bosses play : 36 career busters your supervisor may be
firing your way and how you can defend yourself / Russell Wild.
       p.   cm.
    Includes index.
    ISBN 0-8092-3085-2
    1. Managing your boss—United States.   I. Title.
HF5548.83.W55   1997
650.1'3—dc21   97-17418
                                          CIP

Cover design and interior design by Amy Yu
Cover and interior illustrations by Linda Kelen

Copyright © 1997 by Russell Wild
Published by Contemporary Books
An imprint of NTC/Contemporary Publishing Company
4255 West Touhy Avenue, Lincolnwood (Chicago), Illinois 60646-1975
U.S.A.
All rights reserved. No part of this book may be reproduced, stored in a
retrieval system, or transmitted in any form or by any means, electronic,
mechanical, photocopying, recording, or otherwise, without the prior
permission of NTC/Contemporary Publishing Company.
Manufactured in the United States of America
International Standard Book Number: 0-8092-3085-2

17   16   15   14   13   12   11   10   9   8   7   6   5   4   3   2   1

Contents

Acknowledgments   **ix**

Introduction:
Leveling the Playing Field   **xi**

Part I Games: A Snapshot

1 **The Modern-Day Corporation as Cultivator of Games**   **2**

A Veneer of Civility ▪ The Shifting of Class ▪ The Softening of Big Labor's Belly ▪ Trembling Bosses ▪ Angry Bosses ▪ Bosses of Questionable Talent and Commitment ▪ Diversity Among Bosses ▪ The Mother of All Games

2 **The Contemporary Employee's Role— from Sucker to Swine**   **12**

Paranoids Breed Paranoia ▪ The Gutless Get Gamed ▪ Brutal Bosses Need Permission ▪ Perfidious Personnel

3 **Ten Basic Strategies of Gamesmanship**   **18**

Count to 30 and Try to Figure Out What's Going On ▪ Give the Boss the Benefit of the Doubt ▪ Never Be Needy ▪ Don't Say, "I Caught You,

Sucker!" ▪ Clarify All Objectives ▪ Tend to the
Care and Feeding of the Boss ▪ Get Allies ▪ Forget
About Revenge ▪ Be Assertive from the Start ▪
Study the Sport

Part II A Menu of Games

4 **National Games**:
So Ubiquitous They Pass for Business as Usual **30**

The All-New Reimbursement Program:
Like Pennies from Heaven 31

The Pale Bonus:
You'll Be Sooo Surprised 33

The Firm:
It's a Helluva Place to Work 35

The Grand Bake-Off:
The Most Cooperative Takes All 37

The Glaring Game:
Not for the Fidgety 40

We All Have to Tighten Our Belts:
How Long Can You Hold Your Breath? 41

Trivial Pursuit:
No Misdeed Goes Unnoticed 43

You Bring Colors to Life:
Say Cheese for the Brothers 46

We Simply Had No Choice:
Layoffs as Acts of God 47

5 **Deadly Games**:
Master Them or Face Career Death **52**

The Blame Game:
You Did It 53

The Stolen Credit Game:
  All Your Work for Naught 55

The Pending Promotion Game:
  Hang in There, Chump 56

The Knight in Shining Armor:
  Everyone Will Be Dazzled 58

Squirrel in the Corner Office:
  Sure to Drive You Nuts 59

Carnac the Magnificent:
  What's the Boss Thinking? 61

I Do Everything I Can for You:
  A Game of Misplaced Trust 63

The Leper:
  How Do You Like Quarantine? 65

The Happy Usher:
  Leaving Is in Your Best Interest—Really 67

Night of the Living Consultants:
  Their Presence Is a Mystery, Until . . . 71

6 Dreary Games:
Eating Away at Your Sanity and Career **74**

The Annual Surprise:
  And, Oh, Yeah, Happy Holidays 75

The Harried Executive:
  Whisking Down Hallways 77

Old Poker Face:
  Stoniness as an Art Form 79

Who Can Be the Crudest:
  Words with Hidden Meanings 81

The Cone of Silence:
  This Is Top Secret, Max 82

Monkey in the Middle:
Who Are You Going to Blame?   84

The Game of Life:
Let's Get Philosophical   85

The Oasis Game:
You're Alone in the Desert   87

Jeopardy:
The Category Is Favoritism   88

Suggestions, Please:
All Ideas Are Welcome (to Be Rejected)   90

7 **Overtime Games**:
Keeping You Tied to Your Job Around the Clock   **94**

Gold-Plated Droppings:
Just What You Always Wanted   95

The Kentucky Derby:
Who'll Be First to the Finish Line?   97

When I Was Your Age:
Amazing Feats of Yesteryear   99

Ain't It Terrible We're Understaffed?
A Game of Eternity   101

Face Time:
Where Were You?   103

The Holy Softball Game:
Sundays Are Fun Days!   105

Conclusion:
It's Up to You to Break the Cycle   **107**

Resources for Additional Insight   **111**

Acknowledgments

Thanks to my distinguished experts on organizations and the people who run them: Alyce Ann Bergkamp, Jared Bernstein, Mark Case, Charles Derber, Andrew J. DuBrin, Marlene Elliott, Bruno Gideon, John Gladfelter, Jack Golodner, Robert Gordon, Barry Greene, Laurie Hamilton, Robert Jaffe, William Krieger, Diane Menendez, Michael Mercer, Anthony Mulkern, Linda Putnam, Joel Rogers, David Schnall, Justin Schulz, Michael Shahnasarian, Dennis P. Slevin, Robert Vecchiotti, Alan Weiss, and Frances Bonds-White.

Thanks also to helpful personnel at the American Psychological Association, the American Psychiatric Association, the International Transactional Analysis Association, and Coach U.

Special thanks to my ace reviewers: Nancy and Bob Ippolito, Maria and Alan Tjeltveit, and Susan Wild; to Steve Perrine, my editor at *Men's Health* magazine (where *Games* was first an article); to Ellen Greene, my enterprising agent; and to Kara Leverte and all the other helpful people at Contemporary Books.

Extra special thanks to Jeffrey Kahn of Workplace Associates in New York for his vast professional insight.

And an honorable mention and deepest sympathy to the many dozen downtrodden employees who shared with me their tales of woe.

■ ■ ■

Notice

The games described in this book were culled from a hundred or so interviews with real-life employees. Further details came from discussions with therapists and consultants who work with scores of other employees. Bosses' names, where known, have been omitted or changed to avoid reprisals against the sources. (Many game-playing bosses are big into revenge.) Besides, it's the games that are important here. The bosses themselves are as interchangeable as American lite beers. Any similarity between the bosses in this book and the reader's boss, or any of the author's former bosses, is completely coincidental.

Introduction
Leveling the Playing Field

Walk into any gathering of friends, in any city, at any hour, and you'll hear at least one person grousing about the boss.

Granted, some employees are just complainers, the kind of slackers who spend most of their workday exchanging E-mail with friends, sipping company coffee, and wondering why they can't get ahead. On the other hand, some bosses fully deserve every slur thrown in their direction. These are the bosses who play demolition derby. With your career.

Many boss games are attempts by the insecure to cover up for their own perceived incompetence. Others are the purview of bosses acting as cogs in a corporate wheel greased with greed. And many games come to pass simply out of habit and mindlessness—the boss plays games because that was the behavior taught by his or her bosses, teachers, and parents. All games, or at least those that are discussed in this book, involve deceit for the purpose of intimidation or manipulation.

Getting sucked into a boss's game is no fun. By establishing both the game and the rules, the boss obtains a home court advantage. In certain games (such as The Happy Usher), a boss may even have professional consultants to train and inspire him. But that doesn't mean you can't play the boss's game and win. To do that, however, you need to fully understand the sport and your opponent.

■ ■ ■

That's what the book you have in your hands is all about.

My goal in writing *Games Bosses Play* was to even the odds, to give you, the subordinate, a fighting chance, if not a competitive edge. To give you that edge, I've interviewed several dozen top career coaches—experts in human relations and business—and I've talked to numerous employees who have actually used many of the tactics described. Used right, they work.

So study these games. Be prepared for them. And if you are ever forced into play, play tough. Play to win.

Russell Wild
Rwild@Compuserve.com

Part I

GAMES:
A SNAPSHOT

1

The Modern-Day Corporation as Cultivator of Games

Kelen

As long as there have been bosses, there have surely been games of manipulation and intimidation. Insecurity, greed, incompetence, jealousy, pettiness, shoddy communication skills—the pillars of games—are certainly not inventions of the modern age.

Yet the games played in today's business world, the games outlined in this book, stand out in history for both their sophistication and their breadth. There are several reasons for this.

A Veneer of Civility

The bad bosses of yesteryear—the screaming, demeaning, butt-kicking, outright abusive bosses like Dagwood's Mr. Dithers—still exist, but they have been largely replaced by the subtle, smooth, MBA'd incarnations that make up much of today's management force. The same character defects are still there and still evident. But the manner in which they are manifested has radically changed.

Today's boss is held to a certain standard of "civilized" behavior. A modern boss mustn't yell, wag a fist, or call someone a loser, at least not face to face. Rather, a California-mellow kind of chic has permeated the culture of American business. Any boss who doesn't project mellow generally isn't going to be harvesting a paycheck for long.

In this environment the psychologically haywire boss, the boss who has a need to exercise absolute control, must do so by playing manipulative games. The poor devil has no choice. To protect his career, he must pretend to be something other than what he is—a tyrant. So he'll play puppeteer by glaring at people (see The Glaring Game, Chapter 4), making false promises (see The Pale Bonus, Chapter 4), and telling lies (see Ain't It Terrible We're Understaffed, Chapter 7).

The Shifting of Class

How did all this phony harmony become so much a part of the corporate scene? It's largely a class thing. In the United States, the middle class rose to prominence only in the years following World War II. The current generation, and the bulk of today's workforce, is the first workforce in history to have been predominantly raised in middle-class families. People who come from nice suburban homes grow up with certain expectations of how they should be treated. They expect a certain degree of courtesy and consideration.

"Unlike the poor and uneducated, people raised middle class come to feel a certain amount of entitlement. They are accustomed to getting at least some respect," says Charles Derber, Ph.D., a professor of sociology at Boston College. "Middle-class people also present a potential danger to the company because their education gives them a little influence and power." Many middle-class people, for example, count among their family, friends, and neighbors at least one attorney who knows something about labor laws and civil rights.

Today's boss who manages a white-collar workforce can

no longer get away with outright rude and demeaning behavior. (However, such behavior is not all that hard to find in the basements of hotels, in the kitchens of restaurants, and other blue-collar environments.) Most white-collar employees would openly object to such treatment, resort to the courts, or perhaps commit secret acts of sabotage in retribution.

The Softening of Big Labor's Belly

While today's middle-class employees may have gained certain attitudes about respect as children, they did not inherit their parents' or even their older siblings' bargaining power in the marketplace. Clearly, the leverage that employees gained in the 1950s and '60s started to weaken in the late 1970s, fizzled throughout the '80s, and all but went pop in the '90s.

A look at overall wages illustrates the point. According to statisticians at the Economic Policy Institute, worker compensation in America has stagnated for two decades, *despite* record corporate profits, increased worker productivity (up 25 percent from 1973 to 1996), and longer and longer workweeks (up from forty-one hours in 1976 to forty-seven hours in 1996). At the same time, fewer workers enjoy job security, health benefits have been cut for many, and decent pension plans have all but disappeared.

Economists attribute the weakening of American workers' clout to such diverse factors as the globalization of the labor market, the advent of computer technology, and the swallowing up of many companies by larger companies. And where is organized labor while all this is going on? Shrinking. In the 1950s and '60s (when real income for most Americans was rising steadily), unions embraced roughly 29 percent of the labor force. By 1996 that percentage had dwindled to 15 percent.

Whatever the reasons for American employees' weakened position vis-à-vis their bosses, it is a sad fact of working life—and a big contributor to games. A weakened employee, like an injured mouse, invites the cat to come and toy. "People are much more expendable today, and that has allowed managers much more leverage to mistreat employees," says Andrew J. DuBrin, Ph.D., professor of management at the Rochester Institute of Technology and author of *Getting It Done: The Transforming Power of Self-Discipline.*

Trembling Bosses

Ironically, while the average employee feels extremely vulnerable today, things are often worse for the front-line boss. Middle managers, of course, dropped like fat flies during the great reorganizations of the past decade. If one subscribes to the theory that an insecure boss is more likely to play games—as every expert interviewed for this book eagerly does—then the current corporate environment (here today, lunchmeat tomorrow) is acting like a giant hothouse in which games can only flourish.

"Bosses play games when they feel too threatened to be open and honest, when they fear deep down that they can't cut the mustard," says Alan Weiss, Ph.D., president of Summit Consulting Group, a Rhode Island–based firm specializing in management and organizational development, and author of *Our Emperors Have No Clothes.*

"Cutting the mustard"—achieving career success—for today's middle manager usually means cutting wages, benefits, and personnel while concurrently jacking up subordinates' workloads. Those are the marching orders from above. The manager feels caught in that clichéd locale—between a rock and a very, very hard place. The ugly choices available are to butt heads with those above or manipulate those below. It takes an exceptionally secure person to operate in such an environment without resorting to games.

Angry Bosses

The impetus to manipulate and deceive may come from anger as well as from cowardice. Anger can spring from being forced to treat others shabbily, or it may sprout from being treated shabbily by those above. Or both.

"I'd write up a lot of game playing to displaced anger, and many middle managers today have much reason to be angry," says Dennis P. Slevin, Ph.D., professor of business administration at the Joseph M. Katz Graduate School of Business at the University of Pittsburgh, and author of *The Whole Manager*.

"I know a number of executives who were displaced from high-income corporate jobs, and now they are working elsewhere for considerably less," says Slevin. "Many of these are men and women with spouses who also must work full-time to support the family, which often creates a lot of time crunches and stress."

Many other middle managers have held on to high-salary positions, but at a huge cost, says Slevin. "I talked to one fellow the other day who got repotted into a good job, but he had to relocate to another state, and that meant that his wife had to give up her good job."

Bosses of Questionable Talent and Commitment

In addition to their justifiable insecurities and anger, front-line bosses today may possess less ability than those of yesteryear. Explanation: The huge flux in personnel today gives upper management a smaller pool of experienced employees from which to pick their rookie managers. As a result, the company elders often have to go with any warm body that's been around for a few years (let's call it promotion by attrition), or they hire an unknown entity from the outside. Either way, it's often a mistake.

"Someone coming from the outside into a company as a first-line manager has only about a fifty-fifty chance of proving competent. That's because there's only so much about a person that can be told from a résumé and a set of interviews," says Anthony Mulkern, a seasoned corporate executive who now directs Mulkern Associates, a Los Angeles–based management consultant to several *Fortune* 500 companies, including Eastman Kodak, Hewlett-Packard, and the Adolf Coors Company. Any boss who is insecure about his or her job *and* truly incompetent to boot often turns out to be a virtuoso at playing psychological games.

There are also, says Mulkern, a good number of bosses

today who, all things considered, don't really want to be bosses. In fact, they may resent the added responsibilities. These people happen to be in management positions simply because they had reached the maximum pay limit for their profession (easy as pie these days), and taking on the management role was the only way to wring a decent raise out of their employer.

That person may have been a terrific teacher, engineer, or graphic designer but will not necessarily be a very good (game-free) boss. This is especially true if managing other people's careers is something the professional-turned-boss equates with pain.

Diversity Among Bosses

The arrival in the past few decades of women bosses on the corporate scene has without question contributed to the prevalence and sophistication of office games. It's not that women are more subtle and less direct than men—although they often are. It's not that women know more about psychology than men do—although they often do. Rather, it's the mingling of women and men, with their often vastly different communication styles, that causes misunderstandings, ambiguities, mistrust, and sometimes paranoia. These feelings can lead to a breakdown in open communication, and that can lead to game playing.

"Men and women are like cats and dogs in that they have different ways of communicating. When a dog approaches a cat, even with the best of intentions, the cat will assume the dog is attacking," says Robert Gordon, Ph.D., a psychologist in Allentown, Pennsylvania, who works with many high-powered professionals.

"I'm convinced that neither male bosses nor female bosses use games of deception any more often," says Gordon. Nevertheless, he adds, because of the different styles of communication, female bosses may appear to be somewhat more guileful when seen through the eyes of their male subordinates. And male bosses may be more likely to appear overbearing or deceptive to their female employees.

A similar kind of mistrust can develop where other kinds of diversity exist. For example, an African-American boss, no matter how straightforward and honest, may have a harder time developing or seeing trust among primarily Caucasian troops than a boss with a white face would. We all tend to be more trusting of those who look like us, who went to the same schools and grew up in the same communities as we did. Whenever there is mistrust—no matter who initiates it—the odds of a boss playing games increase.

The Mother of All Games

On top of all else, there is one game so common and so destructive of trust that it results everywhere in the spin-off of other games. We're talking about the gap between what management of late *says* and what it *does* (statements like "Our people are our most valuable asset" versus the cutting of wages and benefits, downsizing, and treating people with disrespect).

Andrew DuBrin calls this "The biggest boss game played today."

Charles Derber says this game creates an environment of mistrust and paranoia quite similar to what was seen behind the former Iron Curtain of Europe. "Many employees in

America today must feel similar to what Eastern Europeans felt living under Communist leaders who would make compassionate speeches yet treat people with extreme harshness," he says.

Let's call this prevailing corporate game the Mother of All Games. From it are born lots and lots of baby games.

2

The Contemporary Employee's Role— from Sucker to Swine

G ame-playing bosses generally don't ask you to join in their deceit. They force it upon you. On the other hand, there are some employees who unwittingly invite games, typically by acting either like paranoiac fools or hapless victims.

Other employees, because they are lazy, unhappy, incompetent, or all three, don't do what they are hired to do. Screw-offs force strong bosses to motivate and educate (and occasionally relieve) them; they force weaker bosses to initiate games. A third group of employees (the swine of the labor pool) will initiate their *own* games, yank the boss in, and then feel resentment and contempt when the big guy doesn't roll over and play dead.

Paranoids Breed Paranoia

Certain employees, given their cynical feelings about all power figures, will perceive manipulation and deceit on the part of the boss even when none is present. That almost always spells trouble. "The problem with approaching a situation as if there's game playing is that it tends to be a self-fulfilling prophecy," says Linda Putnam, Ph.D., an expert in organizational communication at Texas A&M University in College Station.

■ ■ ■

In other words, employees who treat the boss like a manipulator and con artist are often successful at transforming the boss into just that.

For example, Judy the boss asks Bill the subordinate to prepare a report showing the feasibility of starting, say, a new in-house recycling program. Judy is overworked, understaffed, and not terribly organized to begin with. She has no recollection (or perhaps no knowledge) that a preliminary report was done two years back. Bill gets halfway into the project and discovers the report on his own. He assumes Judy knows all about it and is playing a nasty game to undermine his career.

Bill starts talking behind Judy's back. He demands that she put all her requests to him in writing. In his dealings with her, he is cocky and cold. He even runs into Judy's boss in the men's room and makes a sarcastic remark about Judy, which naturally gets back to her. Judy is insecure. She gets nervous. She feels Bill is out to sink her. So what does she do? She starts playing games to cripple Bill's career.

"Some people assume deception when there is merely disorganization. Doing that will cut off the lines of communication. Once communication breaks down, that usually leads to deceit and manipulation," says Putnam.

The Gutless Get Gamed

Nobody's perfect. Nearly all bosses—even the most non-neurotic—have some game-playing potential in them. This is particularly so when pressure is coming from above to make more and more money with fewer and fewer resources. But who among the staff will be the first chosen to participate in the boss's manipulations?

It will be those who advertise their vulnerability. "Generally it pays to do whatever is needed to make the boss happy, but if you're so flexible that you're spineless, then you make yourself a target," says Michael Mercer, Ph.D., an industrial psychologist with the Mercer Group in Barrington, Illinois, and author of *How Winners Do It: High-Impact People Skills for Your Career Success.* "If the boss has any meanness, or any propensity to play games, then the one employee who lacks courage will be the one singled out."

Spinelessness often comes from deep-seated insecurities, usually stemming from childhood. But contributing to poltroonery is the feeling of having few options in the career marketplace. Ultimately, your power to deflect games comes from the knowledge that other job opportunities are always out there, and that if the worst ever came to pass, you could stand up from your desk and parade out the door.

Brutal Bosses Need Permission

Not only are frightened employees the ones most likely to be singled out, they are also the ones who will remain stuck in games that go on and on, like weekend cricket. "Employees get stupid when instead of having some kind of strategy and techniques for dealing with a boss's games, they just shrug their shoulders and put up with them. Passivity only encourages and enables more and more game playing," says Alan Weiss, Ph.D., of Summit Consulting Group.

This kind of enabling behavior in the office, and the mistreatment it may actually inspire, is strikingly similar to the interpersonal dynamics involved in domestic abuse cases, says Robert Jaffe, Ph.D., a psychotherapist in Sherman Oaks, California, who specializes in helping people who have been abused. "In both situations," says Jaffe, "one person (abuser or boss) starts ruling by fear, and the other (abused or employee) buys into it by feeling more and more powerless, less and less in control."

Perfidious Personnel

Not all employees are victims. Quite the contrary. Some create their own games. Motivated by laziness, greed, insecurity, anger, or simply the thrill of the sport, they force bosses into their own webs of deceit, and then may later conveniently forget who initiated the trickery in the first place.

Example 1: Anytime the boss asks Brian to take on a project, Brian says, "I don't know how," or, "My calendar is full," or, "What should I do?" The boss, after a while, gets awfully irritated. In a misguided effort to get Brian to take some initiative and show a little enthusiasm, the boss may wind up playing a psychological game such as Gold-Plated Droppings (Chapter 7) or When I Was Your Age (Chapter 7).

Example 2: The boss asks Kit on Monday to have a project done by Friday. Kit says, "No sweat." She has, in fact, plenty of time. But days pass and Kit does nothing but her nails. On Thursday at 4:30 she tells the boss that she's been working hard all week, but the project can't be done by morning unless she spends all evening cranking. Her agenda: She wants acknowledgment, praise, overtime, or comp time for working late into the night. If the boss discovers what is going on, he may feel that he has to start issuing bogus deadlines or playing the game of Face Time (Chapter 7).

Example 3: Tom attacks Bob the boss for being hostile. He says some very nasty things to Bob in front of several members of the staff. Bob (who really is a caring guy and generally pretty level-headed) gets angry and yells at Tom. Tom points to Bob and says, "See. *See*. That's what I mean. You're screaming at me. That proves how hostile you are."

3

Ten Basic Strategies of Gamesmanship

Kelen

I n any game, there are specific tactics for dealing with particular situations. But there are also basic strategies that
hold true for any and all situations (keep your eyes open
when you hit the baseball; develop your minor pieces before
you bring out your queen; don't shoot for the basket from
center court). The specific tactics for particular boss games
are presented in Part II. This chapter details ten solid strategies you can use anytime, anywhere:

1. Count to 30 and try to figure out what's going on.

2. Give the boss the benefit of the doubt.

3. Never be needy.

4. Don't say, "I caught you, Sucker!"

5. Clarify all objectives.

6. Tend to the care and feeding of the boss.

7. Get allies.

8. Forget about revenge.

9. Be assertive from the start.

10. Study the sport.

This chapter explains how the basic strategies work.

■ ■ ■

Count to 30 and Try to Figure Out What's Going On

Bosses are like snowflakes—no two are the same.

"Your boss, as a human being, has complex feelings and motivations," says Jeffrey Kahn, M.D., a New York psychiatrist who works with executives and is president of WorkPsych Associates, a mental health consulting firm. "Dealing with the boss—and any games he may be playing—will get easier as you learn more over time about the boss's personality and its unique quirks."

Be patient.

Give the Boss the Benefit of the Doubt

"Unless you have hard evidence that your boss is playing games with you, you should never assume that he is," says David Schnall, Ph.D., professor of management and administration at the Wurzweiler School of Social Work of Yeshiva University. "It pays to assume he is innocent, even if it means getting hurt a few times."

In other words, suppose you ask the boss to meet with you to help guide you on a new project, and she hasn't gotten back to you for two days. Try to assume that she is swamped with work or forgot. To assume otherwise—that she is playing games—can get you all flustered for nothing.

Worse, if you proceed as if there is a game, and there isn't, you risk starting a game of your own and possibly ruining what could be a good working relationship.

Even if you think you have reason to believe the boss is

playing a game, remember that most games result from the boss's insecurity or the forces that bear on the boss from above—they are not the result of satanic leanings.

"It is dangerous to adopt the assumption that there's malevolence. You'll make yourself angry. Don't get into mind reading," says John Gladfelter, Ph.D., a psychologist in private practice and faculty member of the Fielding Institute in Dallas.

Never Be Needy

The best defense you have against being turned into a puppet is to have the confidence to cut the strings if you need to. Your employer is not the only employer on the planet. To remain self-assured concerning your employment abilities, it helps to keep your résumé up to date, maintain your contacts with the world beyond (both outside your department and outside your company), and make sure that you are always learning new, marketable skills.

It also helps to walk around with the attitude that you are not an indentured servant, nor even a devoted employee, but rather an independent contractor. Think of your employer as a mere client—your most important client, yes, but still a client. Nothing more. "Your goal is to develop the permanent mind-set that you are independent, very good at what you do, and capable of finding work elsewhere," says California psychotherapist Robert Jaffe.

This attitude will help build your self-confidence, and that will exude from you like perfume in the wind. Merely getting a whiff, your boss will be more inclined to treat you with due respect.

Don't Say, "I Caught You, Sucker!"

Getting roped into someone else's game can make you feel like a big chump. Your first impulse may be to act like the town sheriff, to tell the boss that you see the game, you know what he or she is up to, and the jig is up. Think twice before doing that. If you make the boss look like a fool, feel like an idiot, and sense that you think you are smarter—all of which will likely occur if you publicly expose the game— then you are going to get chopped down at the knees.

"There is a reality to the power the boss has over you, and you need to recognize that. You may not want to stop playing the boss's game if that will result in the boss looking for someone else who *will* play the game," says William Krieger, Ed.D., a private counselor and business consultant in Albuquerque, New Mexico. "You don't want to lose your job."

If you and the boss are particularly close and have a generally honest relationship, and if you are in rock solid at the company, then you may sometimes—subtly and diplomatically—let the boss know that you sense a little game playing going on. Don't be surprised, however, if the boss refuses to see (or genuinely can't see) his or her own game. Bosses often get seduced by their own rhetoric and wind up buying it. For example, a boss playing Gold-Plated Droppings (see Chapter 7) may actually come to believe that offering you a chance to pick up his dry cleaning is a deluxe career opportunity for you. Bosses, like all of us, are also prone to acting out rigid scripts. A boss whose own first boss (or father) played Gold-Plated Droppings may perceive it as proper boss behavior, not a game.

In general, your best course is to pretend that you don't see the boss's games. In *Knots*, his insightful critique of human nature, psychiatrist R. D. Laing wrote, "They are playing a game. They are playing at not playing a game. If I show them I see they are, I shall break the rules and they will punish me. I must play their game, of not seeing I see the game."

Clarify All Objectives

Games, like stars in the sky, can form out of whirling chaos in the universe. When you are uncertain what your boss wants out of you, when your boss is unsure what you want out of him or her, when everyone is showing up to work doubtful of purpose, duty, and expectations, games will arise.

"Ambiguity is at the heart of game playing," says author and business administration professor Dennis Slevin. "Slam the brakes on ambiguity, and most game playing will cease."

How can you, as an employee, do that? "Be very, very clear on what you are expected to deliver," says Barry Greene, vice president marketing and customer service with Astra Merck, Inc., and formerly an associate partner with Andersen Consulting. "Express to your boss what you expect to get out of your job, what you expect to learn and earn. Good up-front definitions will avoid a lot of trouble down the road."

Tend to the Care and Feeding of the Boss

By and large, bosses are not producers. They need others, like you, to do the work. Do it, and do it exceptionally well, and you wield real power. You become a feeder, less likely to have your hand bitten or to be roped into games than a nonfeeder.

"Look for ways to lighten your boss's load," says Astra Merck's Barry Greene. "If you see a situation that allows you an opportunity to pinch-hit for him—say, for example, stepping in to do a presentation in his place, ask to do it. You'll make his job easier. He'll be pleased. And you may have a good learning experience."

The more the boss comes to depend on you, the better.

One caveat: Be careful not to overfeed an overtly insecure boss, particularly one whose career seems to be downward bound, advises psychiatrist Jeffrey Kahn. "Showing too much gusto about taking on a troubled boss's duties may be interpreted as a threat." A boss on rickety ground, if at all prone to paranoia, may think the overly industrious underling is looking to play king of the mountain and shove the boss off his or her turf. You need to avoid such potentially dangerous misunderstandings.

Get Allies

Bosses can manipulate and deceive most easily when employees are fragmented and not communicating with one another. For example, in the case of The Kentucky Derby (Chapter 7), the boss ups your workload because a colleague of yours has proved—allegedly—that the workload can be upped. Touching base with that colleague (who may not be, in reality, quite the racehorse the boss portrayed) may be all it takes to end the game.

In a broader context, employee solidarity gives each employee power, the psychological and economic power to win games or quit them. In that great source of many games—the tussle over the fruits of labor and who's going to keep them, the boss or you—worker organization is key to who ultimately wins.

"Airline pilots need no college education. They work with a tool. So what makes airline pilots highly paid and well-respected professionals rather than mere mechanics? It's because they have an airline pilots' *association*," says Jack Golodner, president of the department of professional employees of the AFL-CIO. Other professional employees who have successfully unionized include teachers, school principals, actors, film directors, nurses, and newspaper journalists.

New unions, more often professional than not, are being formed every day. "Organizing happens in different ways. Usually a bunch of people get together and work with an existing union. The first step is to call a union—any union—and the people there will tell you what you need to know or which other union you should contact," says Golodner. By law, management cannot interfere with your forming a union or punish you for doing so.

Forget About Revenge

The bosses who play the meanest games, the nastiest games, the games that cover up for insecurities and spring forth from neuroses often wind up playing star roles in our sadistic daydreams. Hurt by them, we despise them, and we seek to get revenge.

"Forget it. You don't have to," says Pennsylvania psychologist Robert Gordon. People who initiate nasty, manipulative games are a certain psychological type, Gordon explains. And you don't have to get even with them, for their miserable fate is already sealed.

"They may achieve impressive success in terms of power, title, and material wealth, but it's all overcompensation," says Gordon. "They're not content people with friends, good family, and connections to the community. They tend to suffer from chronic interpersonal problems. In other words, their own personalities are their punishment."

If your boss is an outright paranoid (prone to such pastimes as The Blame Game or worse), you can rest assured that that person will eventually self-destruct. "They all do," says Gordon. For fictional and real-life examples, think of Captain Queeg from *The Caine Mutiny* and former president Richard M. Nixon.

Be Assertive from the Start

As soon as you have hard evidence that your boss has roped you into a game, you need to develop an action plan. Do not allow a game *meister* to work you over while you crouch in the corner with your head between your legs, hands covering your neck.

"Anytime you start feeling and acting like a victim, you're in big danger of being done in," says Los Angeles consultant Anthony Mulkern.

The kind of action you'll need to take will depend on you, the game, the boss, your boss's boss, and the nature of your relationships. Some supervisors can be met head-on; others are better dealt with from the side or behind. Your action probably does not need to be immediate, and in many cases it needn't be drastic. But whatever you do, make sure you don't crouch.

Study the Sport

As long as you have someone you call boss, chances are you will occasionally encounter games. If you have a bad boss, you'll undoubtedly have to deal with many games. You often can't run from them or hide. Even corporate dropouts who become entrepreneurs sometimes discover that powerful clients can play games very similar to those played by bosses. Sometimes the only thing you can do is play.

In his 1964 classic psychology text, *Games People Play*, psychiatrist Eric Berne analyzed the games people play in their daily lives. What defines a game, wrote Berne, are two chief characteristics: "their ulterior quality and the payoff." For there to be a game, there must be deception, and there must be a payoff.

When you are trying to counter a boss's deceptions, a good first step is to figure out his or her expected payoff. Why the "ulterior quality" of your dealings with your boss? Why might you be getting conned? What's in it for the boss? After you've figured that out, the second step is to develop a solid, workable defensive strategy.

In the next section of this book, you will read about thirty-six games played by bosses. Under each game is a description of how the game is played. This is followed by a section called "Game Analysis," where you will find the possible payoffs for the boss. After the analysis comes "How to Play It," a list of suggested defensive strategies.

Keep this book in your desk at work. Use these discussions as your guides, and refer to them whenever you get that itchy feeling that the boss is toying with your career and life.

Part II

A MENU OF GAMES

4

National Games

So Ubiquitous They Pass for Business as Usual

O nly with freak luck will you escape getting sucked into any of the ten games outlined in this chapter. Some, such as The All-New Reimbursement Program, have damned near become American institutions.

The All-New Reimbursement Program: *Like Pennies from Heaven*

It wasn't that long ago that a yearly raise of 6 or 7 percent was as sure as spring rain. This year, your boss offers to cough up a measly 2 percent (keeping you just about even with inflation). "However," he says with a plywood grin, "you're really better off under this new reimbursement program." He goes on to explain that due to the astonishing largesse of the corporate entity, there now exists a bonus system whereby an aggressive soul like you can actually wind up making *more* than under the timeworn system of boring and predictable raises.

Game Analysis

In the past decade, most employers have all but scrapped fixed raises in favor of more volatile, bonus-based pay plans. In those same years, take-home pay for the average worker—despite huge growth in corporate profits, increased productivity, and exceedingly longer work hours—has remained as stagnant as pond scum.

"Giving bonuses in lieu of raises has allowed employers to provide a nice cushion for themselves. Unfortunately, it hasn't worked out to be such a good deal for the majority of workers," says Jared Bernstein, labor economist with the Economic Policy Institute in Washington, D.C., and coauthor of *The State of Working America.*

Why not such a good deal? The main reason is that raises, like diamonds, are forever; bonuses are more like glass. Sure, you scored big this year, but next year you may get shattered. You and yours can find yourselves, like so many American working families, eking by on Hamburger Helper and hope.

How to Play It

- Get self-centered. If your future economic welfare depends more on bonuses than raises, make darn sure that the bonuses are good ones. Argue for rewards linked to your individual achievements, rather than relying on company-wide or department-wide bonuses. Then make certain that your boss is reminded with great regularity of all the glorious things that you do for the company. Keep a written record of your accomplishments, and attach dollar figures to each.

- Work in a consolation prize. "Lousy bonuses tend to be binary—hit or miss," says consultant Alan Weiss. "Try to get the boss to agree that if you reach 80 percent of your goal, you still get 80 percent of your bonus."

- Rally the troops. If the organization is fixed on cutting compensation across the board, you're going to be hard-pressed to make yourself the sole exception to the rule. Your choices are few: shoot for a higher position, walk toward the nearest exit, or work with your colleagues to present a united front, perhaps pulling in a union, as described in Chapter 3.

"Reducing your standard of living is not a fun game to play. The only way to win may be to organize a power bigger than yourself," says Joel Rogers, professor of law, political science, and sociology at the University of Wisconsin.

Some employers may take it personally and get nasty if you try to organize. Laws exist on the books to protect you from retribution—at least in *theory*. In reality, organizing is always fraught with danger (see *Norma Rae*). Proceed with caution.

The Pale Bonus:
You'll Be Sooo Surprised

All year the boss has promised you a "really nice bonus" if you worked very hard. So work hard you did. Many nights you slumped home feeling like overcooked linguine. Here it is December, and you walk into the boss's office with great hopes and expectations. You envision a new pool, a week in the Caribbean, a case of Dom Perignon. . . . You impatiently tear open the envelope containing notice of your hard-earned reward. It's an invitation to dine with the boss at Taco Delight.

Game Analysis

Dangling rewards for desired behavior is a time-honored way that people get others (people, lab rats, etc.) to do their bidding. It becomes a noxious game if the rewards are spoken of often and elusively, with clear exaggeration of their value. "Part of the boss probably knows the bonus isn't going to be that big—he just wants to string you along, and he's got his fingers crossed that you won't ask him to be specific about the value," says psychologist John Gladfelter.

Sometimes employee awards are so ridiculously insignificant that you'd swear the boss was purposely setting out to humiliate you (although that's probably not the case). In one Dilbert cartoon, the boss presents a hard-working employee with a framed piece of pocket lint from a vice president's trousers.

How to Play It

- Eat crow. If you never pinned the boss down on what exactly he or she meant by "really nice bonus," there's not a whole lot you can do right now. "In order for your bonus to be adjusted, someone would have to admit to making a mistake. Don't hold your breath," says industrial psychologist Michael Mercer. So say thank you. Be courteous. Express gratitude (which is not the same as expressing satisfaction). Then make sure your boss can never play this game again. . . .

- Go for the pin. Say something like, "While I thank you for the thoroughly delightful Mexican dinner, next time around I'd like something a little more lasting. What exactly would I need to do this coming year in order to get a $5,000 bonus in December?" Get the boss to commit it to writing, or do it yourself and send him a memo of confirmation, says Mercer.

- Don't be cowed. Be ready should the boss come back at you and say you are being greedy. This is a favorite tactic among bosses trying to withhold money. Simply say, "Yes, I'm greedy, but I worked really hard this year. It took an awfully big toll on me and my family, and I'm hesitant to do it again without knowing that I'm appreciated." By owning up to your "greed," you prevent the boss from using it against you, says psychotherapist Robert Jaffe.

The Firm:
It's a Helluva Place to Work

The boss wined you and dined you. He treated you with great respect. He told you the corporation was "ethical," "supportive of employees," and "a fun place to work." He told you that promotions would come rapidly and every day would bring a new adventure. The reality: You are stuck in a pathetic little cubicle, doing mind-deadening work of very questionable value, and the man who once told you, "We all love each other dearly," never makes eye contact and calls you Fred (your name is Ed).

Game Analysis

A boss who wants you on board may do or say whatever it takes to seduce you. It's awfully difficult to know if what an interviewer tells you is reality, embellishment, or total bunk. "You often see the same kind of untruths in job interviews that you see in the dating world," says Laurie Hamilton, Ph.D., a psychologist in private practice in Asheville, North

Carolina. "You only discern the truth after the courtship is over."

How to Play It

- Next time, get smart. Go in with your eyes open. The interviewer says the company is "ethical," "enlightened," "sensitive," and that raises come "quickly." Ask what the interviewer means by those terms—with examples of each.

- Look beyond the interviewer. Don't judge a company only by what you are told. "When visiting a company, pay careful attention to the atmosphere of the place," says Mark Case, director of the career development office at the Yale School of Management. "Are people talking in tones that are open and friendly, or cold and hierarchical? How are the offices arranged? Are office doors open or shut?"

- Dig up your own contacts. Realize that employers often handpick people to talk with job candidates, choosing those with the sunniest dispositions, rosiest attitudes, and brightest careers. Find your own inside sources. "Work through your college's alumni office to find people at the company who can give you a more neutral, perhaps truer picture of the place," says Case.

- Smell for fear. Ask people you talk with to reveal the worst thing about the company. If you fail to get anyone to say anything bad, that can be a sign people are too frightened to speak up.

- Check the boss's record. If you're particularly turned on by the prospect of fast promotions, there's one good way to gauge just how fast you can expect them: Find out how fast your prospective boss is moving along. "If he's a fast-tracker, getting promotions every two years or less, that's a very good sign. Typically bosses who get promoted pull those under them along," says Michael Mercer. "On the other hand, if the guy hasn't been promoted in years, you are *not* going to be going anywhere fast."

The Grand Bake-Off:
The Most Cooperative Takes All

In every hallway in your place of employment, you find laminated posters with slogans such as "We do things the cooperative way." At group meetings the boss talks incessantly of teamwork. At least that's the rhetoric. In reality, the boss takes every opportunity to pit worker against worker. The place is about as cooperative as a medieval joust.

Around review time, for example, the boss makes it quite clear that there is only a fixed budget for raises—and the budget will stay fixed. Therefore, every dollar raise your coworker gets means a dollar less for you. And every time there's another downsizing, everyone knows darn well that those who aren't logging the serious hours will be the first to be sent to the glue factory.

Game Analysis

"Every manager in the country will say that he's a teamwork-oriented manager. Yet a lot of them don't have any idea what that means. They may have a relationship with the other senior people, or even their own staffs, so they think there's great teamwork—but others below don't even talk to each other," says consultant Anthony Mulkern. "This is ignorance, but it also becomes a game when the boss is going along with the current orthodoxy, spouting empty words, without caring or doing anything to make cooperation happen."

Deep down, below the rhetoric, most bosses don't believe in cooperation or don't think it could ever happen (so why try?), says Frances Bonds-White, Ed.D., psychologist and director of Counseling & Consultation Associates in Philadelphia. "Most managers subscribe to the old divide-and-conquer mentality, that it's easiest to control and manipulate people when they're pitted against each other." Why then all the babble about cooperation? "It became fashionable back in the 1980s in response to the Japanese economic threat. But it's hardly the typical American manager's mind-set," says Bonds-White.

Another, extremely nasty explanation for The Grand Bake-Off appears in recent union literature titled *Working Smart: A Union Guide to Participation Programs and Reengineering* (Mike Parker, Jane Slaughter, et al. Detroit: Labor Notes, 1994):

> Under management-by-stress, teams are never organized to allow workers to gain more specialized skills, but rather to abolish such distinctions. "Team" equals "group of interchangeable workers."

In other words, when the boss informs Tom, Dick, and Harriet that they are now a happy team, the long-term goal may be to have them swap knowledge and skills so that each of the three becomes expendable. This interchangeability can come in awfully handy the next time the boss gets the itch to "downsize" by one worker—especially if the remaining two workers can be convinced to carry the canned employee's full load.

How to Play It

- Volunteer to coordinate. Assume that your boss, at least at some level, wants a certain degree of teamwork but just doesn't know how to make it happen. You throw in your two cents. Say something like, "John, we're aiming for cooperation around here, but I see a lot of back stabbing. I'd like to make some suggestions to help carry out our stated goals." As long as you don't get defensive about it, the boss may actually listen to your suggestions, says Robert Jaffe.

- Be cooperative *and* ambitious. Being cooperative does not mean you have to be self-effacing. Work well with others, sure. But that doesn't mean you can't, or shouldn't, continue to toot your own horn and draw management's attention to your special talents.

- Latch onto the buzzwords. "If the powers that be have determined that teamwork and cooperation will be the fad *du jour*, and it's clear that the boss is only playing a game, then you should just pretend to join in," says Michael Mercer. "You don't necessarily have to do anything different, but make sure that you throw the words *teamwork* and *cooperation* around a lot, especially when reporting on your projects and accomplishments."

The Glaring Game:
Not for the Fidgety

Debate is raging around the conference table as to whether to contract with a new distribution company, stick with the old, or take on the function in-house. You patiently wait your turn, then turn to the head of the table to present what you think is an articulate, intelligent, well-informed opinion. The boss doesn't say a word. She simply glares at you. And glares at you. Her eyes bore into you like bee stings. Finally you restate your opinion, but now you are feeling defensive and starting to sound like a bumbling fool.

Game Analysis

"In the old days tyrants had knives, swords, and clubs with which to intimidate people. Today they glare," says Diane Menendez, Ph.D., a psychologist in Cincinnati, Ohio, who has coached several hundred managers and executives of *Fortune* 500 companies. "The boss is acting like an authoritarian parent who exercises control by glaring at the naughty children."

How to Play It

- Stare—don't glare—back. "Stay silent and open. Recognize that the boss is using a control tactic. Realize that there's a game unfolding and you don't need to be part of it," says Menendez. "Just wait the silence out. Breathe deeply, and silently count to 10 very slowly."

- Don't play psychic. "Most of us, when the boss glares, are going to imagine the worst, like, 'He's thinking how stupid I am,'" says Menendez. "There's no point to your getting all worked up about what the boss may be thinking." First, there's no way for you to know. Second, when bosses consciously play The Glaring Game they're thinking nothing more than how to make you feel uncomfortable so that you will be putty in their hands.

- Name the game, sort of. If the boss doesn't let up, say something like, "You look disturbed by what was said. Perhaps there is something that you need to say?" Be careful with your tone, though. Do not sound challenging. Act as if you are merely curious and concerned.

We All Have to Tighten Our Belts:
How Long Can You Hold Your Breath?

What with foreign competition and deregulation and the rise in the price of papyrus, the corporation is having a tough year, says the boss. He asks for your understanding. Then, with a long face and rueful tone, he informs you that there will be no raise and no bonus for you this year. "Sorry," he says, "but we all need to tighten our belts. You want the company to survive, don't you?"

Game Analysis

Sure, companies sometimes go through tough times. But more often than not these days, the line "we all have to tighten our belts" is used to get employees into accepting pay freezes so that a greater percentage of the company's money can be funneled toward paying shareholders and executive salaries. The result: "Whereas corporate profit rates are at a thirty-year high and top-executive compensation has sky-rocketed, real wage rates for the median worker have seen no gain in twenty years," says Jared Bernstein of the Economic Policy Institute.

At the moment, the uppermost executives of the five hundred largest American companies are raking in roughly two hundred times what the average employee is paid. So chances are that while you are being asked to tighten your belt—which may mean real hardship for you and your family—the top people in your company are living like emperors of Rome.

How to Play It

- Do a little digging. If your company issues public stock, it's easy to find out how well it is doing—just get the annual report. Pick one up at the company's financial or public relations office, or call any stockbroker. You may discover that there's plenty of money rolling in, but that it's all going somewhere other than wages—like into the pocket of your CEO, who just got a million-dollar bonus in addition to a prodigious salary.

- Focus your anger. Don't throw the company report in your boss's face. "Unless you report to the top, chances are the guy telling you to tighten your belt is making only a small percentage more than you are," says Alyce Ann Bergkamp, an expert in organizational behavior at the Catholic University of America in Washington, D.C.

- Write your congressperson. This game is so big that you are highly unlikely to escape it by running to another company. If you've never been a political activist before, this could be a great time to start. At the time this book went to press, Representative Martin Sabo of Minnesota had proposed a bill (the Income Equity Act) that would prevent companies from taking tax deductions on any executive compensation that runs more than twenty-five times the salary of the corporation's lowest-paid worker.

- Buy stock. Become a shareholder in the company for which you work—even if you can only afford to buy one lousy share. That way, at least you can cast a symbolic vote to yank those members of the board who support lavishing all profits on shareholders and top execs, and doling out only crumbs to the people who actually do the work. It will make you feel better.

Trivial Pursuit:
No Misdeed Goes Unnoticed

Things seem to be going swimmingly. You're handling a tremendous workload. You've nailed several large accounts in the past months. You made a knockout presentation to the executive committee only last week. One Friday evening, however, as you're loading up your briefcase with weekend work, the boss appears all snarly-looking in your doorway. He holds a stack of receipts in one hand and starts smacking them against his other hand. "Susan, I just went over your expenses for that Chicago trip. How many times do I have to tell you that I want the damned receipts in chronological order? This is the last time I'm going to tell you. Do you understand?" And he storms off.

Have a nice weekend.

Game Analysis

The boss who foams over trifling details may be compulsive, perfectionist, and by nature a pain in the ass. Compulsive perfectionists often can't stop nitpicking at their own lives and careers. Failing to achieve perfection themselves, they expect it of everyone around them—especially their subordinates. For the insecure boss, picking nits may also be an attempt to show you that he or she is infinitely wiser than you and has more power (*I'm* the Boss).

In many companies today, this is also a game played by bosses who can't or won't give just compensation to deserving people. They exaggerate minor transgressions as convenient excuses for withholding raises and bonuses. A version of this game is often played out at the annual review (see The Annual Surprise, Chapter 6).

If your boss is singling out you and only you for these tirades, there is likely more to it than extreme perfectionism or the greed of the corporation. There's a reason that it's you and not somebody else. The boss probably has a hidden agenda, perhaps a big problem with you that he is afraid to address directly. In a worst-case scenario, the boss may be hell-bent on keeping you down or forcing you out, and is busy building a case against you.

How to Play It

- Use reverse psychology. If you dig around and discover that the boss is persnickety with everyone, breathe a sigh of relief. Then, very diplomatically, try to help your boss see what a turkey he is being. Next time you get jumped on, comment on your boss's cleverness in catching the error and your appreciation for being shown the right way. Do it subtly, and the boss may be a little ashamed to have made such a big stink over such a little thing. But don't push it. Get too gushy, and the boss will sense sarcasm.

- Exude cool. Some bosses play this game just to get a rise out of you. If you fail to burst into flames, the boss will likely find another stick to put a match to.

- Seek higher authority. If the boss is driving you and everyone else absolutely crazy with Captain Queeg–like rantings, complain to his or her boss or the chief of personnel (or the ombudsman, if your company has one). Obviously, you want to do this only if you can trust the person you approach to keep your meeting anonymous. If you can't trust that person, consider an anonymous letter.

- Be proactive. Give a micromanager lots of detail about what you're up to. Having to ask you would likely inflame the boss's temper.

- Get it straight. If you discover that you are being singled out, the first thing you might do is check with friends in your department who may know more than you do. Ask whether they have any ideas why the boss has been so nasty to you lately. "Others often know," says management consultant Anthony Mulkern.

- Smoke out the boss's beef. Say, "I've got a problem here. I don't feel that my performance of late has been pleasing you." Give your boss the opportunity to tell you what's *really* bugging him, advises Mulkern.

You Bring Colors to Life:
Say Cheese for the Brothers

You are asked to dress your best and show your mug at the corporate communications office for a photo shoot. Management wants to put your black or brown face on the cover of a slick new corporate brochure designed to ballyhoo the multiracial/multicultural wealth of the company. You're not surprised they called you. They've done it before. After all, aside from the janitorial staff, you are one of only a handful of non-Anglo employees working at corporate HQ.

Game Analysis

Management in your company may truly be interested in hiring and promoting people of various cultures. If that is the case, they know that minority recruits will most likely be attracted to the firm if some racial diversity is already in place. No game there. On the other hand, the company directors may be more interested in the *appearance* of diversity than in actually doing anything to promote it. If the latter is the case, playing along with their game of deception makes you feel like a fool of color.

How to Play It

- Grab the opportunity. "This is one game you can turn around and use to your advantage. Tell management that you'll be happy to sit for the cameras—just as long as you can help review minority applications," says consultant Alan Weiss. "As part of the recruitment team, you'll know whether minorities are applying, and you can follow up to find out if and why they're being turned away."

- Don't get suckered. As a minority applicant, don't believe all you see in the glossy brochures, says Yale's Mark Case. "In the later rounds of the interviewing process, it's OK to point to pictures of diversity in the recruitment literature and diplomatically ask the interviewer if you can speak to any minority employees." Once you find them, ask about the firm's attitudes and true commitment to diversity.

We Simply Had No Choice:
Layoffs as Acts of God

Sudden layoffs every last Friday of the month have become the norm in your office. These are followed up by Monday-morning meetings at which the department head, looking despondent as can be, eats doughnuts and tells you and your colleagues how deeply sorry she is. The blame, she says, rests squarely on the shoulders of the previous department head . . . the slow economy . . . the board of directors at the parent company . . . rascally consultants . . . the rings of Saturn. You name it. The boss herself claims no responsibility and certainly, she emphasizes, had no prior knowledge. "Gosh, I only learned about this myself last Thursday. I feel terrible."

Game Analysis

There are several boss games often played whenever people are laid off. One is The Happy Usher (see Chapter 5), in which the dearly soon-to-be-departed are guided swiftly and deceptively out the front door. Other games, such as Ain't It Terrible We're Understaffed (see Chapter 7), are concocted by the boss for the benefit of the survivors. We Simply Had No Choice falls into this latter category.

The reason for this game is straightforward enough: Finding a convenient scapegoat is a way for the boss to avoid blame and deflect the aggression of remaining employees who just saw their friends' entire lives shaken. "The boss wants to get off the hook," says management professor Andrew J. DuBrin.

Claiming no prior knowledge is often an integral part of this game. It is how the boss makes excuses for not giving your former coworkers the same notice that management would expect from them, if they were the ones to initiate the divorce. (The boss's rationale is that if employees receive more than a few hours' notice, they are likely to goof off at work and possibly steal paper clips.) One freelance outplacement counselor contends that lack of knowledge is probably a phony claim: "Those who do the laying off always know weeks, if not months, in advance. That's been my experience."

How to Play It

- Look to the future. Once the decision has been made to lay off staff, it's highly unlikely you can change that decision. You don't have to be a Nostradamus, however, to predict the company's next possible move. Get ready. Companies that downsize once are more than likely to do it again. Have your résumé prepared for launch.

- Stuff your anger. There's no way for you to know for sure how big a role, if any, your boss played in the massacre or how soon he or she found out what was going down. Don't assume the boss is necessarily playing a game. Even if you have reason to think so, maintain positive relations. Don't give in to your urge to scream.

For the time being, just bob your head in agreement when the boss says, "We had no choice." You don't want to be on the short list of future casualties.

- Play Portnoy's mother. After the shock has worn off and you feel you can approach the boss rationally, make an appointment to see her. Explain that, given the current work environment, you are concerned about job security. Point out how much you matter to the company—and how much your paycheck matters to your family. Season your boss to feel murderous guilt should she even *think* about including you in the next round of cuts.

- Get people talking. Downsizings most often occur when corporations have no vision. If there were a vision, and if the corporate leaders had any morality to speak of, part of the vision would call for the avoidance of firing people en masse, says psychologist Diane Menendez. To help your company find vision (and possibly spare you from a future downsizing), you might take a lead in helping the company find its way. Step one is to end the game of We Simply Had No Choice. Suggest a meeting, says Menendez, in which everyone—you, your colleagues, and the boss—talks about how they may have contributed to the unfortunate layoffs that recently occurred.

- Work for solidarity. Get people in your department talking about what might happen if upper management demands yet more labor cuts next month. If you can get your colleagues to jibe, you might convince the boss to agree to future pay reductions rather than layoffs. So if the top brass orders labor costs cut by yet another 20 percent, your supervisor agrees that no one will be laid off, but everyone will take a 20 percent cut in pay (preferably offset by a certain reduction in hours). Then, when things get better, salaries and hours can be reinstated. If things don't get better, people can leave for their own greener pastures—at their own schedules.

- Instill a little fear. Don't wait till you've got a pink slip in your hand before going on the offensive. Let your boss know what you would expect in terms of severance if you were asked to leave. Explain that if the company is reasonable, you will respect the firm's intellectual property, cooperate in passing off your assignments, and forever speak only kind words about the company. Pleasantly imply that if the company isn't reasonable, you are going to put up a battle that will make Iwo Jima look like a thumb wrestle.

5

Deadly Games

*Master Them
or Face
Career Death*

M any promising careers have been shattered by one of the ten boss games outlined on the following pages. These are, by and large, the ugliest kinds of boss games, often the productions of the most warped executive minds.

The Blame Game:
You Did It

There you are, sitting at the regular Monday powwow, happy as morning dew, sipping your macadamia-nut coffee, when suddenly all eyes turn to you. The senior VP for operations has asked why the critical new warehouse isn't open, and your boss (who told you to shelve that project) shoves an apple in your mouth and serves you up as the sacrificial sucker.

Game Analysis

"The insecure boss can't admit he's imperfect and therefore can't admit to errors. So when errors do occur, he needs to point a finger. It's that simple," says consultant Alan Weiss. Of course, if the finger lands on you, things can get rather complex.

■ ■ ■

How to Play It

- Take the bullet. You'll do more damage if you try to shift the blame to your boss. Your task is to minimize the bleeding. First, calmly acknowledge the problem, being certain to drop the word *we* in a few times, to suggest that you weren't alone. ("Yeah, *we* really missed the boat on this one.") This sends the signal flying around the room that your department, not just you, screwed up. And who's in charge of your department? Right, your boss.

- Solve the problem. Show everyone in attendance what a solution-focused being you are. Talk up all the things that you (no longer a need for "we") will do to tackle the problem.

- Collect the IOU. Once the storm has passed, say something to your boss like, "Hey, glad I could help out." You're serving a reminder that, by taking a hit for the boss, you delivered—and you expect it returned.

- Practice defensive penmanship. "God created the cover-your-ass memo to deal with the finger-pointing boss," says industrial psychologist Michael Mercer. Having the boss's orders on paper may be enough to discourage him or her into no longer trying to frame you. And if the constant finger-pointing puts your career on the line, these CYA memos may act like Teflon—and keep you from sticking to the frying pan.

The Stolen Credit Game:
All Your Work for Naught

You envision a new product—say, a pedal-powered toaster oven. Your boss calls the project a lemon; it winds up a peach. Next thing you know, the great naysayer is getting slapped on the back for *his* phenomenally brilliant new venture. And you're still pushing paper in your windowless crypt at the end of the hall.

Game Analysis

"Maybe it's jealousy. He wishes *he* had invented the pedal-powered toaster oven," says psychiatrist Jeffrey Kahn. "It's possible that the guy hasn't had a major coup himself in years. Maybe if some young upstart like you gets credit, he sees himself on the way out.

How to Play It

- To anyone who will listen, praise your boss for how supportive he was to you on the toaster oven project. This will let others know—oh, so subtly—that this was your baby. With any luck, it'll also get back to your boss how glowingly you speak of him.

- Demonstrate your knowledge. At meetings with the corporate elders, figure out ways to bring up points about the toaster oven project. Inject fine little crumbs that only an insider could know, advises Alan Weiss.

- Be your own spin *meister*. Shameless self-promotion might be the only way you'll ever get any credit, says Michael Mercer: "Build allies in other departments. Plug your successes. Write articles about your projects for the company newsletter. Create a tidal wave in your favor that will wash right over your boss's head."

- Be creative. There are sneaky but harmless ways to make yourself look more valuable to the company. One young exec—we'll call him Tim—teamed up with Tom, a pal of his in another division. Tim copies Tom on all of his memos; Tom does the same for Tim. This way, each of them appears to have considerable importance in the company. Why else would they be CC'd on so many different subjects?

The Pending Promotion Game:
Hang in There, Chump

All smiles and unbridled optimism, your boss tells you that a promotion is right around the corner. Yessir, it's coming any day now. Of course, you first need to prove that you can handle this new high-responsibility job—on top of your present job. So he dumps on you a walloping load, gives you a wink of the eye, and disappears into the executive mist. You toil away for months on end. Talk of promotion never comes up again.

Game Analysis

As in The Pale Bonus (see Chapter 4), The Pending Promotion Game is played by bosses who feel it is their managerial prerogative to dangle carrots in front of people. In this case, the carrot is a loftier position within the company (and all that it entails). "It's a manipulative technique some bosses play to get people to do their bidding, without having to make a firm commitment," says counselor and business consultant William Krieger.

How to Play It

- Get specifics. As soon as your boss even intimates that a promotion is in the wind, start talking terms. Squeeze the boss into a solid agreement. Inquire, "If I see the XYZ project to its end . . . If I bring in three new clients . . . If I work Saturdays for the next twenty-one weeks—then I'll get my promotion?" If your boss agrees, put it into a memo with his or her name on top.

- Argue for authority. If it's too late for a firm agreement, you may have to lean heavily on the boss to get your promotion. Argue that getting the promotion will help you do the job more effectively. Chances are, that's true. Without the title, the authority, and the budget, you're probably facing real constraints (like people you allegedly supervise laughing at you when you ask for something to get done). The boss is more likely to listen if your focus is on productivity and profits rather than a higher salary and loftier title.

- Taste the baloney. If your boss continues to play this game, you're a fool to tag along. "Making false promises is a pattern for some bosses; it's a character flaw. Once you recognize this flaw, you should stop taking your boss seriously, and don't bank on any of his promises. To do so will only mean that you'll be continually let down," says Alyce Ann Bergkamp.

The Knight in Shining Armor:
Everyone Will Be Dazzled

You're handed a new task, accompanied by the words "This is an important challenge for you." Challenge is right. Not only is it an area in which you have negligible experience, but the budget constraints are almost insurmountable. Once you realize you're in over your head, you ask the boss for some input, but he brushes you off like lint.

Game Analysis

The boss may simply be too sunk in his or her own projects to help you on yours. Or the boss may have the faulty notion that you're in control. However, this behavior also may indicate a boss who is playing a game of career chess—with your career. In that case, you can expect one of two moves:

Knight takes pawn. You screw up; everything is about to blow. The boss vaults in like Sir Lancelot—demonstrating to higher-ups how swift he is and how no one (least of all a weenie like you) could ever possibly replace him.

Knight retreats. Your boss doesn't jump in (having never believed in this project). When it fails, his oracular nature is confirmed.

Either way, he comes out shining.

How to Play It

- Look for outside expertise. "If you're in trouble and the boss isn't helping, request help elsewhere—from someone in the firm considered the authority on whatever your task involves," says Alan Weiss. If the authority agrees to help, you receive the guidance you need. And your boss—aware (because you've said so) that the ultimate expert is on your side—can't easily ambush you. In addition, you may get extra credit for your resourcefulness and independence.

- Start scribbling. Get your requests to the boss in writing. Spell out what resources you need. Assure your boss you will give the project your all, but that his or her input is essential. Should the boss's shenanigans one day put your job in check, a collection of illuminating memos may save you from checkmate.

- Advertise the boss's game. "In the corporate world, there are ways of planting information so that it gets back to your boss's superiors without having your name on it," says psychologist Diane Menendez. She suggests subtle mention of your boss's game to older (well-connected) employees in the company, executive secretaries, and office managers who work close to the brass.

Some boss games are, of course, sanctioned by upper management (see, for example, The All-New Reimbursement Program, Chapter 4). Not so for games like The Knight in Shining Armor that risk putting a damper on profits. Advertising shenanigans in these cases could lead to the boss's replacement or reeducation.

Squirrel in the Corner Office:
Sure to Drive You Nuts

In this basically savage, rodent-like version of The Knight in Shining Armor (the previous game), the boss gives you a new project and wishes you success—but knowingly withholds from you information or resources that could be crucial to your achievement.

Game Analysis

There's no question that the boss is toying dangerously with your career. As in The Knight in Shining Armor, the boss may be counting on you to go belly-up so that he or she can stride in, take over the project, and look like a champion. Your boss may, for whatever reason, be looking to eliminate you. Another possibility is that the boss is withholding information as a kind of demented test, to see if you will jump through rings of fire.

"I used to play this game so that people would have to prove they were loyal to me, on my team, dedicated and committed enough to get the work done in spite of the handicap I created," laments Marlene Elliott, twenty years ago the young, insecure manager of a federally funded education program, today a personal coach in Summit, New York, who teaches people to be more effective and happy at work and at life.

Yet another possible explanation is that the boss is withholding information as a way of safeguarding a position of strength. "Some high-powered managers believe that holding back on information makes them more powerful," says Justin Schulz, Ph.D., president of Applied Behavioral Science, an organizational and management consulting firm based in Greenwood Village, Colorado.

How to Play It

- Have a semi-heart-to-heart with the boss. Don't tell her that you suspect she's playing a game, says Elliott. But you can say something like, "I have a sense that there's something else about this project you may not be telling me. I'm not saying consciously, but perhaps subconsciously. I don't know, maybe this is silly. But do you think that I could be right? Is there anything else I should know?" Look for the classic signs of lying, like tapping fingers on the table.

- Question your assumptions. If the boss denies having any more information to give you (and says so without finger tapping, lip biting, and avoidance of eye contact), reevaluate your assumption that there's a game at play. Many bosses know far less than their employees give them credit for.

- Get tough. If you continue to collect evidence that your boss is playing this game, start documenting it. If you have hard data to show that your boss is yanking you around, go to your boss's boss and calmly present your case. There are rare circumstances where going directly over the boss's head is justified. This may be one.

Carnac the Magnificent:
What's The Boss Thinking?

"I want you to do an analysis of our sales force and determine whether there are adequate personnel for the job. Have it on my desk in two weeks," instructs the boss. "No sweat," you reply. You come back in two weeks with your freshly printed report. The boss picks it up, gives it a quick eye, and says, "Nope, this isn't quite what I was looking for. Go back and do it again." So you come back in several days with another freshly printed report. And the process repeats itself. At no point does the boss offer any clear guidance that will help you determine what exactly you are supposed to do.

Game Analysis

As with fluctuations in the stock market, there are countless possible explanations for why your boss can't or won't communicate clear directions. One possibility is that he isn't yet certain about precisely what needs to be done. Or perhaps the boss does have an idea but doesn't want to stick his neck out. The most evil and corrupt motive is that your boss is waiting for you to plow your own way and will then take the credit if things go right (see The Stolen Credit Game, Chapter 5) or pass the whole thing off as your lamebrained idea if things go awry (see The Blame Game, Chapter 5).

Carnac the Magnificent is also played by bosses who are simply trying to kill time. "The boss may not be ready to focus on your project at the moment. Or he may not have a next assignment for you yet. So he's just trying to keep you busy in the meantime," says Astra Merck's Barry Greene. "Some bosses feel that as long as all the plates are spinning, things are good."

How to Play It

- Rephrase your questions. Instead of knocking your head out asking the boss, "What do you want?" and getting evasive answers, ask for a description of how the boss envisions the final outcome, says Greene. For example, instead of asking, "How do you want me to analyze the sales force?" ask, "What outcome do you see as a result of this report?" or "How might the results of this report affect the sales force?"

- Call for a huddle. "Ask the boss to set aside an hour to really brainstorm your project. That will force him to focus directly on it. More times than not, he'll be thankful to have the opportunity," says Greene.

- Spread your efforts thin. Come back to the boss with not only one option, but three or four—and don't spend a whole lot of time or effort on each.

- Write follow-up memos. Every time the boss picks an option, clarifies a point, or sheds any clues whatsoever as to what you should do, put it in writing. That will make it more difficult for the boss to come back later and tell you that what you did was all wrong.

- Get the cards on the table. If you sense the boss is giving you busywork, ask if maybe you could work on something else, says Greene. "Make a suggestion for an alternative project. It's a good opportunity to move into something you might enjoy."

I Do Everything I Can for You:
A Game of Misplaced Trust

You have a big project waiting for budget approval that must go through several committees. Corporate policy dictates that you sit tight and allow your boss to champion your cause. He tells you that he is 100 percent in your corner and will do everything he can to see the project come to pass. But the only thing that passes is time. And more time. And you start to wonder whether the boss is really in your corner or on the opposite side of the ring.

Game Analysis

Perhaps your boss doesn't want to face conflict—which would inevitably result from criticizing your project. Or maybe your boss doesn't have the gumption to back your proposal or the power to affect it one way or another, and is too embarrassed to admit it. The worst-case scenario is that your boss fears you're a lot smarter than he or she is, and is paranoically bent on holding you back, to avoid one day reporting to you.

How to Play It

- Bolster the boss's confidence. Subtly let the boss know that backing you won't make him or her look like a fool. To do this, you need to develop an informal network of allies whose names you can drop on a regular basis. On Monday, for example, you tell the boss, "I just talked to José in marketing, and he thinks we have a pretty good idea here." Later that week, mention that you've also talked to Adrienne and Carol in two other departments, and they think it's pretty nifty, too. (If José, Adrienne, and Carol happen to be higher up the totem pole than your boss, then your problems are long gone.)

- State your puzzlement. If you suspect your boss is out to sabotage you, you must eventually make eye contact and inquire about it, says psychologist Robert Jaffe: "In a nonconfrontational way, say to the boss, 'I believe you when you say you're in my corner, but I'm having a hard time understanding why . . . (give a specific example of how the boss could have helped you, but apparently did not).'"

- Then arrange for regular meetings to discuss your projects and progress, counsels Jaffe. "Just asking for consistent meetings—telling the boss you're going to be looking him squarely in the eye once a week—should start to end the sabotage."

The Leper:
How Do You Like Quarantine?

The workload keeps getting bigger. Budgets are cut. Pay is frozen. A new policy removes all flextime. You talk to several of your colleagues, and everyone is angry. Finally, you've had enough. You make an appointment to see the boss, determined to speak your mind. It's the first time you can remember that you've ever complained to her about a thing. You believe you handled the meeting well, but you're in for a shock. Before you even make it back to your desk, she's telling everyone in the Western world that you are a whiner, a chronic malcontent, a radical, and that no one should listen to anything you say.

Game Analysis

Your boss may favor the policies that you object to or may hate them but is powerless to act because the marching orders are coming from above. The one thing she doesn't need or want, however, is open revolt. She figures the best way to squelch an uprising is to impeach the credibility and reputation of any potential opposition leaders (a workaday strategy of political candidates). So she takes the first person to call things as they are and maliciously labels that person psychologically unbalanced.

How to Play It

- Appeal to the boss's ego. Make another appointment. Tell the boss that somehow you fear you've developed a negative reputation around the office. Make no mention whatsoever of the role she played in spreading that reputation. Ask her to please help you. Get her to view herself as a competent manager tied to solving your dilemma. Convey the idea that if you get out of your predicament, you will have confirmed the superiority of her intellect.

Once you're out of the leper role, make sure you don't ever wind up there again. The next time you wish to challenge corporate policy, follow these guidelines:

- Speak softly. "Sometimes, to effectuate change, a little well-placed emotion can help. But there's also over-emotion, and you need to be extremely careful about that," says Barry Greene, of Astra Merck. "People who shout and scream are easily labeled as lepers."

- Define the issue. Give yourself a day or two to clear your head of angry thoughts, then clarify in your mind what is really bugging you. "Clearly defining the issues can be 80 percent of the battle," says Greene. "You need to know the issue backwards and forwards before solving it."

- Present solutions. "Don't ever go into the boss's office with just a problem. Go in with a problem *and* answers," advises Greene. Say your department's workload has just been increased by 30 percent. Instead of beefing about it pointlessly, suggest to your boss the possibility of outsourcing, pulling help from another department, or increasing bonuses for the staff. Ask, "How can we make this work?"

- Pick your battles. "All of us have only so much capital with the boss. Don't spend it on the trivial," says consultant Anthony Mulkern. No, you never want to become a zombie in a suit, obediently doing whatever you are told. On the other hand, you can't fight every directive from above. If you feel that you must, you're undoubtedly in the wrong place.

The Happy Usher:
Leaving Is in Your Best Interest—Really

It seems like just another Friday afternoon. But on this particular Friday afternoon, the boss hands you a blue folder. Inside is your exit visa to the Land of Unemployment. After six years at the company, you—and a host of your colleagues—are being "let go."

The boss offers you ten minutes of consolation in which she explains that the company needs to do this, that there really are no alternatives. She gives you a brief explanation of the company's "generous" severance package (which you can read at your newfound leisure when you get home), and then comes the coup de grâce: She asks you to clear your desk by three o'clock.

All of this is done in a rather chipper tone. The last thing you remember is a surreal smile and the boss's hand on your shoulder as you're leaving her office. "This is what's best for you, really. Trust me," she says, as if ushering you into the orchestra section of life. It all happens so incredibly fast that you pack your belongings, head for the door, and walk out into the sunlight feeling dazed and confused.

Game Analysis

The way you feel is exactly the way the boss wants you to feel—disoriented, stunned, unable to make decisions, unable to speak. It's not that she's heartless and cruel. It's that she's been well trained. "Companies have been getting extremely sophisticated at terminating people. They bring in professionals—people expert in this—and they teach managers a lot of psychological manipulation," says Boston College professor Charles Derber.

The goal of the manipulation is to avoid bad blood, especially any bad blood that could lead to a lawsuit. Bosses are told that if they play the termination game extremely well, you may actually walk out feeling grateful to the company.

In most cases, bosses are also all too ready to rush you out the door for their own personal comfort. "Firing people is the worst thing managers have to do. They risk anxiety and depression. If they can get you out without a ruckus, they can avoid a lot of uneasy emotion," says consultant Justin Schulz.

How to Play It

- Be prepared at all times. You never know these days when you're going to meet The Happy Usher. You must have an exit plan in effect at all times. Keep your contacts always warm, and the ink on your résumé always fresh. "Otherwise, when the day comes, you'll feel weak and helpless. They'll hit you on the jaw and throw you outside, and your only response will be to say, 'OK, just don't hit me again,'" says Alan Weiss.

- Smell a rat. "Always—always—be suspicious when anyone makes a decision allegedly on your behalf without consulting with you first," says Schulz. So when you hear the words "this is in your best interest," spring up and take notice. The game of Happy Usher has officially begun. Go on to the next step.

- Consider an appeal. "Most people consider a layoff notice some kind of official stamp. But you can appeal it, and some employees are successful," says Michael Shahnasarian, Ph.D., psychologist, outplacement counselor, and executive director of Career Consultants of America in Tampa, Florida. Go to your boss, your boss's boss, or any other senior official within the company with whom you have a relationship, he advises. Argue that laying you off is not in the firm's best interest. Explain why. See if you can get your layoff notice annulled. You have nothing to lose.

- Before you decide to walk, take provisions. Negotiate and negotiate hard for the best severance package you can get. Whatever the pay they're offering, demand that they make it considerably more. Insist on an office and phone for as long as it takes to land a new job. Assert that you need extended health coverage for the same period. You may have to back down on some of these, but your opening demands should leave lots of room to negotiate. Near the top of your list of demands: Make sure you get a glowing letter of reference.

- Flex your muscle. What leverage do you have as they're sending you sailing out the door? "Plenty," says Alan Weiss. "Your boss wants you to go calmly and quietly, and she'll pay up if need be to see that happen. . . . You can threaten to write letters to the editor, complain to the Better Business Bureau and the chamber of commerce, and rally your friends and colleagues." You can also say "Look, if any clients/customers/suppliers should happen to contact me in the future, I'll say only good things about the company" (implying that the opposite will hold true if the company doesn't meet your demands).

- Threaten to drop the bomb. The biggest, meatiest threat of all is a lawsuit. Are you being let go for failure to perform duties that were never part of your job contract? Could your firing in any way be related to a disability, including your being overweight? Could your dismissal somehow correspond to any negative feelings management may have about skin color, religion, ethnic background, gender, age, or sexual orientation? Is it possibly related to your union activities or your talk about wanting a union? Any of these may form the basis for a lawsuit. "If I was told I had an hour to leave the company, I'd spend it on the telephone," says law professor Joel Rogers. "I'd get in touch with a labor lawyer or a union, describe the circumstances, and see if I had a cause of action."

- Seek strength in numbers. Even more frightening to the boss than a single employee bringing a lawsuit is

the prospect of facing multiple proceedings. "Immediately get in touch with others—everyone else who has been booted out or might be booted out," suggests Rogers. "Tell them, 'I was just smiled out the door, and I don't find it very funny. I won't be around for very long, but here's my home telephone number. Get in touch with me. I'm going to do some investigating. We may have a court case.'"

Night of the Living Consultants:
Their Presence Is a Mystery, Until …

This game is a variation of The Happy Usher (the previous game), but rather than lay off a chunk of the staff herself, the boss hires a consultant—or more commonly a team of consultants—to do the dirty work for her. She obviously

doesn't want to tip her hand before showing her cards, so when the consultants arrive on the scene, they are not introduced as outplacement counselors. "These ladies and gentlemen are here to study our business and suggest ways we can work more efficiently," is typically all you will hear—until the day of reckoning. On that day, the boss will escort you into the office of one of these consultants, and this contractor will be the one to tell you how sunny the skies are and how everything is going to be just peachy keen outside the front door.

Game Analysis

There's a parallel here to the wily husband or wife who plans to dump the spouse and asks for marriage counseling to ensure that someone will be around to hold the jilted party's hand at the bitter moment of separation. So it is in Night of the Living Consultants. The consultants are there to hold people's hands. Management hopes to assuage any anger among the staff that could lead to sabotage, morale problems for the survivors, and—most frightening of all for management—costly lawsuits.

Sometimes the consultants themselves (just like the marriage counselor in the last paragraph) are dupes, says business psychologist Justin Schulz. "They come onto the scene actually thinking that they've been hired to improve efficiency, but their real role is to serve as executioners." Management may prefer to keep them in the dark to ensure secrecy and maintain cooperation and control.

How to Play It

- Look to the past. Does the company have a history of hiring consultants to do its dirty work? Do the con-

sultants hanging around your office ever do outplacement work? It's easy to find out. Take a run to your
local library and check out the *Consultants and Consulting Organizations Directory* (Gale Research).

- Look to the future. If you suspect that an earthquake
is coming, suggests Schultz, corner one of the consultants and ask, "How are you going to measure
improvement in efficiency around here?" If the consultant gives you a crisp, clear answer, you can probably relax. But if the response is a zombie-like stare,
indicating possible ignorance or deceit, you'd best get
your fine china packed. The trembling is about to
begin. Review the recommended steps for The Happy
Usher.

6

Dreary Games

Eating Away at Your Sanity and Career

A boss who has discovered one of the ten games in this chapter will rarely grow tired of it. Unless you do something to end the gaming, you will find yourself being toyed with again, and again, and again.

The Annual Surprise:
And, Oh, Yeah, Happy Holidays

It's late December. You stride into your annual review feeling confident and cool. Why not? Profits are up, problems were solved, goals were met—hey, you're a comer. So why the look on the boss's face like he's passing a kidney stone under the desk? Then he starts. One minor client has griped that you haven't returned her phone calls; you failed to pull in one low-priority account; and your absence at the Christmas shindig was, frankly, disappointing.

Game Analysis

Why the Chihuahua bites when the boss should be stroking you and forking over a serious bonus? Perhaps the boss has no choice. Many companies' annual review forms *require* managers to lob in at least a few negatives, says psychiatrist

■ ■ ■

Jeffrey Kahn. Other companies may not specifically demand negatives, but they dictate that only a certain percentage of employees in any department can get a decent rating, leaving it to the manager to invent excuses for holding people back.

On the other hand, your company's annual review policies may have nothing to do with this behavior. You may have a boss who genuinely gets frazzled by little things but, being a procrastinator (or a wimp), has failed to tell you sooner. Another possibility is that your boss is delivering a sucker punch, finding any rationale possible to justify a minimal raise or bonus—because the leaner your department's expenses, the better the boss looks, and the juicier his or her bonus.

How to Play It

- Refocus the conversation. One generally helpful strategy is to wait for the boss to shoot the BBs, then reply, "Look, I think there's a bigger picture here. Perhaps we can talk about the many things that have gone right this past year."

- Document your disenchantment. Often you'll be asked to sign off at the bottom of your review form, and there will be a space for comments. If you don't like your performance rating, state your reasons. Get it on record.

- Demand more feedback. Make sure you tell the boss how surprised you are to hear these criticisms for the first time during your annual review. Explain (calmly) that in the future you'd appreciate more timely feedback. Suggest regular meetings to discuss your work. How's the first Tuesday of each month?

The Harried Executive:
Whisking Down Hallways

The boss is busy, busy. Constantly running down the hallway, checking his watch, darting off like a bull with a dag-
ger in its shoulder. He never has time to sit down and chat.
Assignments are given on the fly. Feedback is minimal to
zilch. Conferences in his office (including your last annual
review) are interrupted by phone calls, during which you sit
patiently and try to look busy reviewing your notes and
studying the office flora. Staff meetings usually involve a
dozen people practicing their sitting skills while they wait
twenty minutes for a sweaty boss to come barreling in
through the door.

Game Analysis

Some bosses choke themselves with work to avoid dealing
with people—subordinates, colleagues, friends, children,
spouse—and all the niggling complexities of human interac-
tions. Others equate bustling behavior with importance,
status, and self-worth. Certain bosses play The Harried Executive in an effort to sell others that they, too, should be
working every waking moment: "What do you mean, you
can't work this weekend? *I* work every damned weekend."

How to Play It

- Pull out your calendar. If you must have the boss's
  attention, you may need to agree on a committed time
  slot during which the two of you can sit down and
  talk. Next time the boss brushes you off, say, "If now
  is not a good time, I understand, but how about next

Thursday at eight o'clock?" Your boss will be so impressed you suggested eight o'clock that he will certainly make the time to see you. (It doesn't matter whether it's A.M. or P.M.

- Nurture the gatekeeper. A good relationship with the busy boss's secretary can often get you access that your colleagues could only dream of having.

- Give positive feedback. Express appreciation for your boss's attention and role as a mentor. Mention that your boss's coaching is crucial to your career success. "Feeding the boss's vanity is all part of what some people call 'managing up,'" says Yeshiva University's David Schnall.

- Write out your request. If getting an audience with The Busy One is impossible, you may need to send your queries in memo form. Be gracious and friendly. Write, "Please forgive the formality of this memo, but I really need your input on this project." Then list all your questions. "It's difficult to kiss off a written memo," explains Schnall.

- Stand up. Should you be whiling away an afternoon in the boss's office while he fields phone call after phone call, there's no problem with suggesting (quickly, between calls) that the meeting be rescheduled. In your most pleasant and mannerly voice, say, "This obviously isn't a good time for you, and it is really important to me that I have your full attention. Can we reschedule for a more convenient time?"

Old Poker Face:
Stoniness as an Art Form

You're sitting in a meeting with the boss, sharing your joy in nailing the biggest account of your career. The boss doesn't exactly look enthusiastic, he looks more like someone watching a public toilet flush. Later that day, you tell him what you think is a pretty good joke, and he looks at you like you're the wall. The man is colorful as tar, as expressive as a dairy cow, without a hint of emotion. You can't remember the last time he smiled or showed the slightest sparkle. At most, on very rare and special occasions, you might get a vague, noncommittal grunt of possible approval.

Game Analysis

If your boss is only a sourpuss around you, you're in trouble. He doesn't like you. If he's pug-faced around everyone, then it's more likely a sign of succumbing to the pressures of the job. Or he may be in the midst of a bitter divorce or root canal surgery.

Putting on a poker face can also be a game. In that case, the boss is doing it for the same reason that poker players do. Many poker-faced bosses figure that they're going to be more successful at manipulating people if no one can read them. "Some bosses fear that if they look happy, for example, people will see how good business is, and they'll start asking for raises," says psychologist Robert Gordon.

Other bosses put on the poker face because they want to look serious and stern in a way that communicates their

alleged superiority. Chances are that someone, perhaps a former boss or their father, taught them that that's what bosses
are supposed to do. "They think looking dour is a way to
frighten the troops into action. It communicates what they
see as the seriousness of command. They associate a friendly
face with laxness," explains Jeffrey Kahn.

How to Play It

- Probe gently into the boss's psyche. "Most of us are
  going to assume that a cranky boss doesn't like us—
  whether or not that is true," says former exec Marlene
  Elliott. "It's OK to ask the boss what's up," she adds.
  "Say to the boss, 'Listen, so that I don't assume that
  it's me, is there a reason you haven't been smiling a
  lot?'"

- Let it be. If the boss tells you that his or her lack of
  verve has nothing to do with you, trust that reply—
  and get on with your life. "Don't dwell too much on
  the boss," advises Kahn. Your boss is entitled to walk
  around with a plaster face. Try to ignore it. Concen-
  trate on your job.

- Go fishing. If the boss's poker face gives you no clue
  what's happening in the company or the department,
  go elsewhere to get your information. "Want to know
  how profitable things are? Date someone in account-
  ing," quips Gordon.

Who Can Be the Crudest:
Words with Hidden Meanings

In the middle of a conversation—any conversation—your boss typically manages to drop in the word *fuck* at least a couple of dozen times. It doesn't matter what the topic of conversation is, or what his mood is, or whether you ever respond in kind. You can't figure it out. Both his parents were English teachers, he graduated from an Ivy League school, he never drinks anything stronger than Snapple, and on weekends his choice activity is putt-putt. Why in his meetings with you does he talk like a character out of a Quentin Tarantino movie?

Game Analysis

"*Fuck* is the most common word used in corporate America today," says a senior vice president in the entertainment industry. When it's used by bosses around their subordinates, it is often part of a game. Using profanities is one way for a guy with a six- or seven-figure income and a home on the hill to show he can "get down with the boys."

This can be an awfully patronizing game. "It's as if the boss is saying, 'Well, I know you people don't have many adjectives, so I guess I'll have to say 'fucking this' and 'fucking that' in order to communicate with you," says Robert Gordon.

It can also be a power game. "Crude language is a way

that some bosses establish 'pissing rights.' It's like the boss is decreeing that he can say 'fuck' because he is the boss, but you can't say 'fuck' because you're only the subordinate. It's a way for him to establish his dominance," explains Gordon.

Coming from a woman, profanity is very often a way of expressing power, says Marlene Elliott. "I used to do it for effect," she adds. "It was a way to prove I was one of the guys. I also didn't mind that it tended to make people uncomfortable. That was my way of saying, 'I'm better, more powerful and important than you.'"

How to Play It

- Be yourself. If the boss's words really offend you, it's OK to express that to the boss. Most bosses will make an effort to curb their tongues. Unless you are really offended, however, just shrug it off. Asking a boss to watch his or her language may get you excluded from the inner circle.

- Don't respond in kind. "Let the boss use all the profanity he wants, but don't jump in and start gutter talking yourself," advises Gordon. "The boss may take it as a challenge to his territorial rights. If that's the case, he could start looking for other ways to establish his dominance. You definitely don't want that."

The Cone of Silence:
This Is Top Secret, Max

You're in the boss's office. He stands to close the door, turns, and lowers his voice for effect. "I want to talk to you in private," he says. You feel like Maxwell Smart joining the Chief of Control under the Cone of Silence. The boss continues, "I just wanted to let you know that Steven (a buddy of yours) is really not pulling his weight." You start feeling kind of queasy.

Game Analysis

Hey, we all need someone to talk to. Maybe you should feel honored that the boss chose you. Alternatively, you could be getting yanked. "Often a boss will invoke the name of an allegedly troubled colleague to exert pressure on you," says consultant Alan Weiss. "He doesn't want to tell you outright to sweat harder, so he plants this coworker into the picture, with the implication that if you don't bust butt, you'll be in dire straits, too."

The boss could also be playing a game that mind experts call *splitting*. "It's how some people deal with emotions, like anger. Instead of going after someone directly, they try to vent their anger by playing one person off against another," says psychiatrist Jeffrey Kahn.

How to Play It

- Open your ears. "There may be a lot of unrecognized anger on the boss's part, and you don't want to mess with that. If The Cone of Silence is what makes him feel less angry, you don't want to lift the cone and enhance that anger. It might be best to just let him speak," says Kahn.

- Don't get sucked in. Be a model of the kind of openness you'd like to see around the office. In the previous example, you might say, "Did you tell Steven he's going down? If I were him, I'd want to know."

Monkey in the Middle:
Who Are You Going to Blame?

You've *begged* the boss for another hand in your department. "I'd love to help," he says, "but I can't." His superiors, you're told, have nixed all new hires for the next twelve months. "I'm powerless," he says. As you're leaving his office, you recall that those were his very words when he told you he couldn't promote you or give you a raise.

Game Analysis

Your boss may be telling you the truth, says Kahn. Another possibility is that he or she lacks the grit to directly turn you down. Or your boss may just not want to hurt your feelings by telling you, for example, that you're not promotable because you're too ugly. Either way, you're not getting what you want, and you're not sure why.

How to Play It

- Determine your boss's position. It's hard to know when the boss is playing the monkey, says Robert Vecchiotti, Ph.D., president of Organizational Consulting Services of St. Louis. You can ask straight out: "Do you agree with this policy?" If he says yes, then at least you know where you stand.

- Call his bluff. If the boss says he's on your side but there's little he can do, you can introduce your own little game. "Well," you say to your boss, "If you feel the same way I do, what say you and I go talk to your boss together?"

- Do an end around. Say to the boss, "Look, I have a problem with this policy, and it's really unfair that you're stuck in the middle. May I talk to your boss directly?"

The Game of Life:
Let's Get Philosophical

You've been slaving for a year. The quality of your work has been superb, and incontestably so. The company's profits are soaring, and your department is revving. So you pump yourself up before your annual review, planning to ask the boss for a hefty raise—and expecting him to agree wholeheartedly. As soon as you bring up the subject, however, the boss gives you a patronizing hand on the shoulder. "You know," he says, "there's more to life than money. Aren't you happy doing the work you do? Isn't that more important than just money?"

Game Analysis

All pigs eat corn. Farmer Jones eats corn. Therefore, Farmer Jones is a pig. By a similar sort of backasswards reasoning, the boss says money isn't that important. You're asking for more money. Therefore, you are an imbecile. In any case, the boss is hoping that you're not up on the science of reasoning and the art of verbal contortion.

How to Play It

- Know your worth. Before arguing for more money, you should know what your talents demand in the marketplace. The easiest way to find out is to hand your résumé to a few headhunters and ask them what they think. With this information, you'll be better prepared to deal with The Game of Life—and any other games intended to keep you working for peanuts (see also We All Have to Tighten Our Belts and The All-New Reimbursement Program, Chapter 4).

- Do a verbal tango. Show your boss how to *really* twist words, courtesy of Swiss business executive Bruno Gideon:

  You: Look, I agree with you, there is more to life than money—and this job offers me a lot in terms of those other things. That's exactly why I want to stay—which is why we need to talk money.

  The boss: So if I can't pay you more, you're leaving. Is that what you're saying?

  You: No, if that were the case, I wouldn't even discuss this with you. I would just leave. But here I am, discussing this. That's why we need to discuss money.

- Bend a little. If the job truly does offer a lot more than money—if it is a fun place to work, the hours are reasonable, and management shows you respect—take this into serious consideration before solidifying your demands for more cash. "There *is* more to life (and work) than money. I know lots of people who make fat salaries but hate what they do," says Astra Merck's Barry Greene.

- Focus on nonmonetary benefits. If your boss can't cough up extra bucks (this may truly be out of your boss's control), then focus on other, nonmonetary perks, suggests Greene. "Consider educational opportunities (like courses at nearby universities), getting on special projects with good people, and attending seminars."

Author's note on seminars: Think San Antonio or Honolulu in the winter, Seattle or Montreal in the summer.

The Oasis Game:
You're Alone in the Desert

A new set of office policies removes whatever flextime you once had. Everyone must be in by 8:30—no exceptions. In addition, all work orders will have to be signed in triplicate by a squadron of supervisors. And the vending machine at the bottom of the stairs now contains nothing but beef jerky (the boss's favorite). During chats in the halls, you infer that others are as irate over these new policies as you. You go to the boss to express this, and the boss says, "Whazza matter with you? You're the only one to complain."

Game Analysis

Your boss may be telling you what he or she truly perceives. You may work with cowardly colleagues who kvetch only outside the boss's earshot. On the other hand, the fox may be using a very common—often successful—manipulative technique. Psychology experts call it *normative pressure*. By telling you that you are "the only one," your boss is appealing to that wimpish slice of your psyche that would rather die than be labeled an outsider or, worse, a complainer.

How to Play It

- Don't get suckered into debate. That will only escalate matters, says consultant Robert Vecchiotti. "Rather than debating, simply tell him that you are taking a leadership position and choosing to talk to him candidly about something *you* perceive as a problem."

- Use diplomacy. Don't label the policy as "the stupidest, lamest, most idiotic thing" you've ever heard of. The boss may take that personally. Employ discretion. Describe the policy as something you as an individual are unhappy with. Period.

- Remember to say thank you—even if you don't get your way. It's to your advantage to make the dander settle. Say something like, "I realize that you may not be happy with what I'm saying, but I appreciate your letting me come in here and share my thoughts." This may allow you the opportunity to come back and voice your opinion, and perhaps initiate change, another day.

Jeopardy:
The Category Is Favoritism

A new position opens up in your department. Allegedly, you're doing the hiring. The boss, however, has a prime candidate to "suggest" to you. "Yep, my wife's nephew, Gregory, would make a darn good addition to your team. Darn good," says the boss. Last month, after you were put in charge of purchasing the office's new phone system, the boss "suggested" that you call Telemaxxx—the phone installation company owned by his golfing buddy, Joe. Now every time you go to make an outgoing call, instead of a dial tone you get something that sounds like a small wounded animal.

Game Analysis

Welcome to the famous old-boy network. If you're lucky, you can contract guys like Gregory and Joe, make the boss happy, and do minimal harm to the company or your personal integrity. If you're unlucky, Gregory turns out to be dumber than dirt, and Joe's phone system is a technological turkey. In that case—ta-da—there you are, a contestant in Career Jeopardy. Either serve the boss by giving these losers a deal, or do what you think is right and put yourself in jeopardy of incurring the big guy's wrath.

How to Play It

- Don't assume too much. "Nine-tenths of the time, the boss just wants to make sure that his buddy is being heard. He doesn't necessarily expect you to break all the rules," says Barry Greene. "I'd suggest that you absolutely talk to the person he's asking you to talk to. Just talk."

- Share your objectives. Outline for the boss the kind of things you'll be looking for in the ideal candidate. Let your boss know what factors will drive your decision.

- Be neutral. Evaluate the boss's chum as you would all others, and then present your findings squarely. If the boss's candidate is bad news or doesn't fit where you're going, state your conclusions dryly and politely. ("I'm afraid that Frank's software package isn't the best quality we could get for the money.")

- Engineer a counteroffer. Maybe Frank could supply *part* of the package?

- Face reality. If you've presented your best case, and the boss wants the friend to get the deal regardless, then you have to either give in or do battle. Calculate how big a battle the boss is likely to wage and how badly you might get bloodied. "It should be a pretty serious issue for you to go up against the boss," says Greene.

- Negotiate something for yourself. If you're going to be doing the boss a favor, at least make sure you get something *you* need, like more resources for your department. ("Sure, Boss, I'll be happy to purchase Frank's software package. But, you know, it's not the quickest thing out there. I think we're going to need a few more computers to use while the existing ones are tied up churning data. And we could use another two offices to accommodate those computers, too.")

Suggestions, Please:
All Ideas Are Welcome (to Be Rejected)

Your boss stresses that ideas are always welcome. As if to prove it, there's a suggestion box right outside her office door. At the bottom of that suggestion box, however, lies a black hole, into which all suggestions drop into eternal nothingness. And suggestions made directly to the boss are killed faster than gnats sucked into a jet engine.

Game Analysis

Has your boss also initiated a "Morale Day"? Has she set up a "Fun Committee"? Where morale is high and people feel appreciated, there's no need for such bunk. In companies that are coercing people to take less money, work more, and shut up about it, managers often seek to pacify by putting on a big show. They try to give the impression (to the staff, and often to their own bosses) that they are enlightened, "participative" managers. In such a circus, you are certain to find the game of Suggestions, Please.

The game is also played by bosses with huge inferiority complexes. Their goal is to prove that nobody knows more than they do. By asking for your suggestions and getting nothing but "worthless" ones back, they "prove" to the world that no one can help them. Inferiority feelings also breed martyrdom—and those "bad" suggestions serve to "prove" that people don't care enough about the boss to help.

How to Play It

- Talk facts. You suggest, for example, that the company might attract brighter job candidates if it occasionally ran employment ads in the *New York Times* rather than in the backs of comic books. The boss says, "Too expensive." At this point, your best response is to ask, "How much do you think it would cost?" Your boss may think it costs a lot more than it actually does—and you can provide the facts. "Hard data will confound him," says psychologist Frances Bonds-White.

- Document the game. Next time a brainstorming meeting rolls around, suggest to the boss that one person write everything down on a big sheet of paper. (If possible, try to get someone else to volunteer.) The note taker should create two columns: Suggestions and Objections, including space to mark down *who* is suggesting and objecting. The object is to subtly show the boss that he or she is playing a game—and that everybody in the universe knows it. At the end of an hour, your sheet should begin to look something like this:

SUGGESTIONS	*OBJECTIONS*
Part-time work availability (Sue)	Not possible (Al)
Casual day once a week (Sam)	Not important (Al)
Higher employee bonuses (Bev)	Not feasible (Al)
Dental coverage (Ross)	Not practical (Al)
Better doughnuts (Jeff)	I eat cookies (Al)

- Recycle ideas. If you propose anything novel to the boss, you're going to face rejection and frustration. If you withhold suggestions, you'll be accused of being a nonparticipator. Seemingly you're in a jam. There's one way, however, to slip out. "When the boss asks you for a suggestion, say, 'Gee, that's a tough one. What are your thoughts on the matter?'" suggests Yeshiva's David Schnall. "After she tells you, edit her words a bit, and feed it right back to her." If you do this suavely and edit just right, you'll wind up getting rewarded for your brilliance, the boss will feel like an extraordinary leader, and everyone can go home more or less happy.

7

Overtime Games

*Keeping You Tied to
Your Job Around the Clock*

Has your existence outside of the office dwindled to breathless minutes between dry cleaners and kids' birthday parties? Your boss has undoubtedly mastered one or more of the following games, and it's high time you take some strong remedial action.

Gold-Plated Droppings:
Just What You Always Wanted

You're already juggling more than a full workload. Today the boss comes at you with yet another project, featuring hours of tedious arithmetic interspersed with stuffing envelopes. By no stretch of the imagination is this project challenging, educational, or fun. Instead of calling the project what it is— grunt work that minimum-wage clerks (now unemployed) used to handle—the boss says, "You're darned lucky. This is an ab-so-lutely golden opportunity for you to learn and grow on the job." With that, he slaps you on the back, hands you a mountain of papers, and heads off to play golf.

Game Analysis

"It would be real nice if all bosses would just acknowledge that not all work they delegate is a 'challenge' and an 'oppor-

■ ■ ■

tunity,' but some bosses feel that they need to polish turds,"
says consultant Robert Vecchiotti. Why? Some bosses take
themselves for potent manipulators and really think they are
hoodwinking you into accepting a "gift." Others are embarrassed, knowing full well the heftiness of your workload and
the skimpiness of your paycheck.

How to Play It

- Add a double coat of plating. When the boss hands you
  those papers, smile and say, "I would take on this project even if it weren't that important." This accom-
  plishes two things, says William Krieger. "First, you're
  inviting the boss to feel awfully good about you. If you
  have to do the work, at the very least get maximum
  credit for it." Second, says Krieger, "you're letting the
  boss know that you know what's going on—sort of."
  Your boss will be dazzled by your intelligence and
  diplomacy.

- Learn dominoes. Right after you've so gracefully
  accepted the venture, if the corporate hierarchy and
  your conscience allow, look for someone else to dump

it onto, says industrial psychologist Michael Mercer. *You* don't have to gold plate it.

- Pull the boss into the act. If you can't re-delegate and the "golden opportunities" keep coming, you may have to rebel. "If you just keep absorbing additional work, the boss will keep dumping it on you, and you'll become the office sponge," says Alan Weiss. Start by asking the boss to help you set priorities, and then leave on the back burner anything that isn't a priority.

If the boss says that everything is a priority, respond with, "Gee, boss, I can't seem to get it all done. Can you help me to better manage my time?" Your object here is to back the boss delicately into a corner. Show the boss that you have five projects on your plate, and they're all due by Friday, and each one should take at least ten hours. Make him or her say, "Oh, that Frutzfinger project needn't take more than two hours." That way, says Weiss, if the Frutzfinger project gets turned in a little undercooked, you can remind the boss about having directed you to devote only two hours to it.

The Kentucky Derby:
Who'll Be First to the Finish Line?

"This project really shouldn't take more than three days," says the boss. "Three days?" you ask, having no idea where on earth such an estimate might have come from. "Er, this is one awfully large project. Don't you think, like, maybe *four* days might be more appropriate?" (You're really thinking *five* days, but you've already been cowed.) And the boss responds, "Nonsense. Sam (name said with a tone of immense adoration and immeasurable respect) took not even three days on a similar project."

With that said, the two-horse race between you and Sam will begin (the boss hopes).

Game Analysis

If your boss has children, it's a sure bet that each one gets to hear how the *other* one is the perfect little angel. This, of course, annoys the hell out of the kids, just as his slobbering references to Sam annoy the hell out of you. The boss's intent, however, usually isn't hard to figure. It's an effort to "motivate" you by getting your competitive juices flowing, perhaps trying to shame you into feeling that you are a laggard.

The boss in this example probably also knows that the time frame he's suggesting is unconscionable. So, rather than have you think of *him* as the devil, he sets up Sam. *Sam* is the one setting the unreasonable standard. *Sam* is the one who does this project in less than three days. *Sam* is therefore the evil one here. It often works.

How to Play It

- Never say you're sorry. If you admit that you're a laggard, the boss has you. "Generally speaking, it's a bad move to give excuses for not living up to someone else's expectations," says psychologist Laurie Hamilton. "It will usually come off sounding like 'The dog peed on my homework.'"

- See the bright side. "Take the boss's time estimate—whether it's based on Sam's work or wherever it comes from—and treat it as the first move in a negotiation," suggests consultant Anthony Mulkern. "Remember that in negotiation, the first person to present a number is usually at a disadvantage."

- Focus on quality. Say to the boss, "Listen, I don't want to do just an average job (implying that that's exactly the kind of work he gets from Sam); I want to do an outstanding job. Isn't a project as important to the company as this worth the time to be done right?"

- Be saintly. If the boss invokes Sam's name so often that you feel you must respond, proceed carefully. As much as you loathe Sam for making life so trying, now is not the time for free expression of hatred. Rather, say something like, "I really admire Sam's ability to work so long and hard. He's quite unique."

- Get corroboration. Say to the boss, "Isn't Sam wonderful? How does he do a project like this in less than three days? Hey, let's go ask him." Talking to Sam, you may discover that "less than three days" was actually more like two weeks, that Sam's project wasn't as complex as yours, and that Sam had two other people helping him out.

When I Was Your Age:
Amazing Feats of Yesteryear

As in The Kentucky Derby, this is a variation of a very common game played by parents. With their children, it sounds like this: "I used to walk ten miles to school, in the snow, uphill both ways." When played with employees, the game sounds slightly different: "When I was doing your job, a project of this sort would have taken me half the time it's taking you."

Game Analysis

Your boss may be experiencing false-memory syndrome or, more likely, is purposely decorating his or her own accomplishments to put the screws on you and get you to devote yet more of your life to the corporate mission. Another possibility is that your boss is acting out feelings of inadequacy. "It's a behavior often seen in five-year-olds. In effect, the boss is making a muscle for you, and he wants terribly for you to go 'Ooooo!'" says psychologist Robert Gordon.

Yet another possibility is that the boss feels resentful because your rise in the corporation is seemingly coming too easy. "This kind of resentment was often felt by women bosses back in the 1970s. They figured that *they* had to trail-blaze the way so that other, younger women could climb the corporate ranks—and that those younger women weren't grateful enough for the fact," explains psychologist Frances Bonds-White.

How to Play It

- Massage your boss's ego. "The boss wants you to acknowledge the great feats he achieved. Do it. He'll likely see you as very perceptive," says Gordon. Don't be afraid to lay it on thick. He'll be nothing but enraptured with your buttery words.

- Don't ever question the past. "Suggest that the boss may be embellishing, and you're going to engage in a pissing contest in which you'll lose," says Gordon.

- Bring things up to the present. If the boss follows boasting with the implication that you, too, should be able to jump buildings in a single bound, you'll need to set the record straight, says William Krieger. Reply, "I really believe you were able to do such a project in a day, but the world was different then. In today's environment, it's going to take me three days."

Ain't It Terrible We're Understaffed?
A Game of Eternity

Your desk—never mind your spirit—is sagging from the weight of labors undone. Yet another overstuffed folder arrives every day. "Hang in there," says management. "What with Rudy leaving last week, and Andrea the month before, we're a little short on people at the moment." Yeah, it's true that turnover has been heavy. But that's been true for at least three years now, and you suspect—given the ever-increasing workload and the motionless salary scale—that yet more stressed and angry employees will head for calmer pastures. And management will continue to promise full staffing.

Game Analysis

Cutting the workforce (either by laying off people or by just letting them leave and not replacing them) is a very fashionable way for management to reduce costs and raise short-term profits. As long as you and your coworkers think the situation is temporary, management is likely to get a fat bonus, because you're more likely to work regular overtime with no added compensation. "The message 'We're temporarily understaffed and there's so much that needs to get done' creates a kind of war mentality in which people are often willing to suffer," says Laurie Hamilton.

How to Play It

- Don't shoot the messenger. Unless your boss is an uppermost-echelon manager, he or she probably has little control over the situation. Chances are good that your boss is as overworked and frustrated as you are.

- Calendar in your social life. Tell your boss that you are willing to help, sure, but just not this weekend. "Unfortunately," you explain, "I have nonrefundable tickets for a weekend in Pago Pago."

- Bargain for comp time. The boss says you need to stay till midnight every day this week? Fine, do it if you must. But somewhere around Wednesday after the sun sets, ask if it would be OK to take an extra day or two off at the end of the month. Just as soon as your boss agrees, pull out your memo pad, put your agreement in writing, and make social plans that can't be broken.

- Suggest trade-offs. The boss may insist that you do a three-person project by yourself. You agree but ask to skip the weekly marketing meeting, get some secretarial help, and perhaps even put in a bid for a new, faster computer. "Negotiate not only time, but priorities and resources as well," advises Anthony Mulkern.

- Try reason. You can argue with your boss that forcing three people to do the work of five is fundamentally unfair. Forget it. That kind of argument and $3.50 will get you a large cup of café au lait. On the other hand, if you argue that the quality of the product is being adversely affected, you have a chance.

Face Time:
Where Were You?

Explicitly, implicitly, and every other way, the boss has made one point perfectly clear: He expects you to be around the office sixty-plus hours a week. It doesn't make a difference what the workload or your level of productivity or the quality of your effort. It certainly doesn't matter that your kid has the flu. All that matters is that you show your face early in the morning and parade it again after the setting of the sun. Face Time bosses are famous for arranging "crucial" meetings at 8:00 A.M. on Mondays. They also love to make the rounds at lunchtime, leaving little sticky notes on the back of your chair that say, "I need to see you. Stop by my office the second you return from lunch."

Game Analysis

You are likely dealing with a boss who has the emotional maturity of a toddler. "For a two-year-old to know that mom exists, mom must be present. I deal with many powerful people who are emotionally two years old. They have to see you there in the office to know you're working," says Robert Gordon.

In addition, most Face Time bosses are insane workaholics. They tell themselves that working seven days a week is proof positive that they are good spouses, providers, and/or corporate citizens. In truth, they are using work as an excuse to avoid intimate relationships, which make them nervous. Deep down somewhere, a Face Time boss knows this. It's this living a lie that makes such a person want the whole world to be constantly at work. "When people are shaky about their beliefs, they have to proselytize, just like religious zealots," explains Gordon.

How to Play It

- Use smoke and mirrors. Get in early and work late, but slip out several times during the day (when you know the boss is in meetings) to do the things you wouldn't otherwise have time for, like food shopping and exercise. Send the boss voice mail and E-mail from home during the wee hours to give the impression that you never stop working. Negotiate to "work at your home office" (which sounds better than "working at home") as often as possible. Do whatever it takes to give the impression that you're working monstrous hours without actually having to do it.

- Find out what makes your boss tick. If playing hide-and-seek gets draining, the two of you may need to have a chat. Do *not* declare what a sicko your boss is. You'll merely convince him that you are a sloth, and you may jeopardize your career. (Besides, the neglected spouses of Face Time bosses already tell them every day what sickos they are.) Rather, express admiration for your boss's work ethic and diligence. Get your boss to start talking about his or her sources of motivation and personal (screwball) values.

  "You're looking to find a window within the rationale," explains Robert Gordon. For example, suppose your boss starts to mutter something about putting bacon on the table . . . and all those welfare slobs who suck off the fat of the government . . . blah, blah . . .

and how what this nation needs is a rebirth of good old-fashioned *family values*. Eureka! You have your window. The next time you want to leave at a reasonable hour, explain that you really, really want to stay, but that you've already put in sixty hours this week, and your passionate sense of *family values* dictates you go home and spend at least a little time with the children.

"How can he argue with that?" says Gordon.

The Holy Softball Game: *Sundays Are Fun Days!*

"Hey, Bob, see ya Sunday!" says the boss as you're leaving Friday afternoon. Yeah, you're thinking to yourself, chucking a softball around with Mr. Big is really what you want to do with your weekend. But you're afraid not to show. Those around the office who seem to have the bounciest careers happen to be regular attendees of these frolicking events. Those who shun them tend to suffer rather anemic careers.

Game Analysis

For some bosses, the truly narcissistic ones, making weekend plans for employees (poker games, picnics, bird-watching expeditions, yoga retreats) can be a means of proving to themselves how much they are adored by their subjects. Other bosses arrange extracurricular activities because they think it's a way to get employees to know each other better, and so boost morale. "They want their employees to be one big, happy family," says Catholic University's Alyce Ann Bergkamp.

That boost to morale might actually occur if there were no strings attached, Bergkamp adds. But the game-playing boss can't help but yank strings. If you don't attend, you are deemed a non–team player. Worse, the insecure boss may decide that you don't like him or her. In either case comes potential retribution.

How to Play It

- Get the scoop. "If you haven't been around for a long time, find out from the old-timers just how important it is to attend these extracurricular events," suggests Bergkamp. "To some bosses it may really matter; others won't deem it that important."

- Decline with finesse. If you don't want to go, tell the boss how sorry you are, but that you have other plans—and be sure to say what those plans are: *to catch up on work*. "If the stated reason for not coming is to devote yourself to work, the boss may respect you more for not showing than for showing," says Bergkamp.

- Come and play badly. If the boss is a competitive softball, golf, or racquetball player, you have an easy out. "Just start missing balls," says psychologist John Gladfelter. "He'll find a way to give you back your weekends."

CONCLUSION

It's Up to You to Break the Cycle

A number of the readers of this book will someday, if they haven't already, get a crack at that glittery corner office. When your day comes, will you have what it takes to be a game-free leader? Or will you wind up doing unto others as your bosses have done unto you?

Social scientists say that abused children, by some strange process of psychological osmosis, are the most likely to become abusive parents. "It may also be true that abused employees are more likely to become abusive bosses," says Yeshiva University's David Schnall. If the professor's hunch is right, you will need to break a rotten cycle. And that probably won't be easy.

Eminent psychiatrist Eric Berne wrote that transcending games ultimately is achieved by three means: Awareness (an ability to see the games); Spontaneity (to rise above the programming of the past); and Intimacy (which affords something more rewarding than games). He wasn't talking specifically about boss games, although these three tools are still perfectly apt.

Awareness. Having read this book, you are already sufficiently aware of the kinds of games that some bosses play. Beware that you don't follow suit or create new games entirely of your own imagination. Analyze your own behavior. Ques-

■ ■ ■

tion your motivations. Strive to be honest with yourself at all times. Seek open feedback from others so that you remain self-aware. Find other bosses who don't play games, and emulate them.

Spontaneity. Don't do things a certain way simply because that's the way they've always been done before. Make certain that all of your rulings make sense, are fair, and humiliate no one. Look to game-playing bosses (parents or teachers) as negative role models; ask yourself how you can do things differently than they.

Intimacy. No, you don't have to hug all your employees as they walk into the Monday-morning staff meeting. But do share your thoughts and your knowledge openly. Encourage experimentation. Ask for ideas from other people—and put the best into action. Model cooperation and open communication. Hire others who seem open and kind. Respect all employees and their private lives. Think of yourself as a manager of projects, not people. Never refer to yourself as anyone's "boss." Think of others as working *with* you, not *for* you. Be generous with praise. Show that you care.

For the psychologically well-balanced reader, much of this behavior will tend to come naturally. The biggest challenge will be remaining open and honest in an organization where managers are encouraged or even coerced into being secretive and deceptive.

Let's say you're a manager told of impending layoffs, but your division VP insists that the rank and file be kept in the dark until the day of reckoning. Or suppose that you and your fellow managers are given colossal bonuses, days after your subordinates were denied all raises with the explanation that times are tough and the company doesn't have a dime to spare. What do you do?

At times like these, you'll need to remember what it was like when you were subject to the games bosses play. Then decide: Which is more important, protecting the status quo or safeguarding your integrity?

Only you can decide.

Resources for Additional Insight

Additional Books About Bosses, Games, or Both

Adams, Scott. *The Dilbert Principle.* New York: Harper Business, 1996. Here, as on your daily newspaper's cartoon pages, Adams captures the raw essence of managerial meanness and madness.

Berne, Eric. *Games People Play.* New York: Ballantine Books, 1964. Reveals the secret games we all play every day of our lives.

Bing, Stanley. *Crazy Bosses.* New York: William Morrow & Co., 1992. A hilarious insider's view of business "bureaucrazy."

Derber, Charles. *The Wilding of America.* New York: St. Martin's Press, 1996. Everything you always wanted to know about greed.

deVries, Manfred F. R. Kets, ed. *The Irrational Executive.* Madison, CT: International Universities Press, 1984. A group of psychoanalysts puts American management on the couch.

Dominguez, Joe, and Vicki Robin. *Your Money or Your Life.* New York: Viking, 1992. What to do if bosses' games drive you to the wall.

■ ■ ■

Downs, Alan. *Corporate Executions.* New York: AMACOM, 1995. A former henchman comes clean.

Hornstein, Harvey A. *Brutal Bosses.* New York: Riverhead Books, 1996. If Stephen King were to write a book about bosses, it wouldn't be any scarier.

Laing, R. D. *Knots.* New York: Vintage Books, 1970. A severe little book that examines the roots of misunderstandings and deceit.

Lewis, Michael. *Liar's Poker.* New York: W. W. Norton & Co., 1989. Manipulation, machismo, and gluttony on Wall Street.

Miller, James B. *Best Bosses, Worst Bosses.* New York: Summit, 1996. Vignettes from real folks about real bosses.

Sweeney, John J. *America Needs a Raise.* Boston: Houghton Mifflin, 1996. Organized labor's modern-day manifesto.

Weiss, Alan. *Our Emperors Have No Clothes.* Franklin Lakes, NJ: Career Press, 1995. A catalog of stupid boss behavior.

Wright, Lesley, and Marti Smye. *Corporate Abuse.* New York: Macmillan, 1996. The truth and consequences of in-humanity in Big Business.

Movies That Feature Game-Playing Bosses

The Caine Mutiny (1954). Captain Queeg paws little balls and goes wacko over some missing strawberries. A perfect example of Trivial Pursuit (see Chapter 4).

Citizen Kane (1941). Charlie Kane runs publishing empire and copes with a rotten childhood by toying with people's lives.

Crimson Tide (1995). Nuclear sub commander can't deal with dissension in the ranks, blows his top, and the world almost goes with it.

Disclosure (1994). Demi Moore finds yet *another* excuse to disrobe—this time it's all part of nasty office politics.

Glengarry Glen Ross (1992). A group of hapless real estate agents find themselves caught in the boss's cruel sales contest.

Mister Roberts (1955). James Cagney is the grouchy and erratic ship's captain.

Mutiny on the Bounty (1935). Mr. Bligh profits greatly from his position while bringing misery to all below him.

Nine to Five (1980). Three secretaries foil the boss from hell.

Wall Street (1987). Wheeler-dealer plays yo-yo with both the stock market and the life of a young protégé.

Working Girl (1988). A wily executive gets her just deserts.

About the Author

Russell Wild grew up on Long Island, studied economics in college, went on to get a master's degree in business, and entered Corporate America, where he worked diligently for years in banking, publishing, and sales. He regularly writes articles for national magazines and has authored and coauthored numerous books, including *Business Briefs: 165 Guiding Principles from the World's Sharpest Minds* (Peterson's/Pacesetter, 1995). He lives in Allentown, Pennsylvania, with his wife, Susan, an attorney, and their two children, Addie and Clay. Before becoming self-employed, he had both good bosses and bad.

■ ■ ■